AN PARÓISTE MÍORÚILTEACH

THE MIRACULOUS PARISH

ROGHA DÁNTA SELECTED POEMS

Poems copyright © Máire Mhac an tSaoi, 2014
Introduction © Louis de Paor

For permission to reprint or
broadcast these poems write to

Wake Forest University Press
Post Office Box 7333
Winston-Salem, NC 27109

ISBN 978-1-930630-68-0
Library of Congress Card Number 2014933129

Designed and set in Verdigris
by Nathan W. Moehlmann,
Goosepen Studio & Press

Printed in the United States of America

First published in Ireland
by The O'Brien Press
and Cló Iar-Chonnacht

Wake Forest University Press
WWW.WFUPRESS.WFU.EDU

THE *An paróiste*
MIRACULOUS
míorúilteach PARISH

ROGHA DÁNTA SELECTED POEMS

MÁIRE MHAC AN TSAOI

IN EAGAR *ag* LOUIS DE PAOR
EDITED *by* LOUIS DE PAOR

WAKE FOREST UNIVERSITY PRESS

AISTRITHEOIRÍ TRANSLATORS

Celia de Fréine (CF)
Louis de Paor (LP)
Gabriel Fitzmaurice (GF)
James Gleasure (JG)
Aidan Hayes (AH)
Valentine Iremonger (VI)
Biddy Jenkinson (BJ)
Máire Mhac an tSaoi (MM)
Eiléan Ní Chuilleanáin (EC)
Douglas Sealy (DS)
Peter Sirr (PS)

i gcuimhne ar Phádraig de Brún

CLÁR CONTENTS

BROLLACH PREFACE

I OWE MY DEEPEST THANKS to all who have participated in this enterprise, including of course our hoped-for readership, but perhaps most of all to the wonderful medium I was privileged as a child to absorb, the Irish language of Corca Dhuibhne. I remember a distinguished Celtic scholar saying, 'When a Dunquin man has said something to his satisfaction, it is poetry.' It is a standard I may not have achieved, but it is the one I aspire to. God rest the many gifted souls who tutored me!

Poets are notoriously bad critics, especially of their own work. I am, however, on fairly safe ground in saying that a major thrust in all poetry is the will to communicate. In so far as this purpose is mine, it has been immensely strengthened by the generosity and grace of my translators. Between us, they, my publishers and I may hope to have accomplished a worthy purpose, that — to adapt the words of wicked old Mr Milton — of demonstrating that we inherit, in the Irish language, 'something that future generations will not willingly let die'. God bless the craft and all who sail in her!

In a sense my poetry is a journal; each effort seeks to stabilise the emotions of a given circumstance, whether the presentation be dramatic or lyric. I have found this facility a powerful resource in times of trouble. Yet another reason to be grateful! In the nature of things the poems treat of many kinds of love, and in this context it is important to realise that love of language is a passion like any other. Writing verse is an addiction, a rewarding one. Perhaps I should leave it at that and trust that so many willing interpreters will have made these points better than I could. Coimrí Dé orthu go léir!

MÁIRE MHAC AN tSAOI
Mullach Bheann Éadair
Samhain 2010

RÉAMHRÁ INTRODUCTION

Others, more competent than myself, have commented on Miss Mhac an tSaoi's technical accomplishment and her sympathy with the genius of the Irish language. This Irish poet has learnt her trade. But what makes this book so exciting is more than the writer's care for form, and its evidence of pride of craft. Miss Mhac an tSaoi has a poetic voice with its own unmistakable timbre, and what she has to say adds up to an unrigged vision. She is a lyrical analyst of the stresses laid by time and human incapacity on love and friendship in their growth, blossoming and withering.

— JOHN JORDAN, *IRISH TIMES* 23 FEBRUARY 1957

BEFORE SHE HAD EVER PUBLISHED a book, Daniel Corkery, whose presence, according to Seán Ó Ríordáin, even popes might enter apprehensively lest they be found wanting, had delivered a positive verdict on Máire Mhac an tSaoi's work. In a 1953 essay on the poem 'Inquisitio 1584', he noted with approval the author's technical accomplishment, her familiarity with tradition, and the graceful simplicity of her language. Three years later, in his Christmas round-up of recent publications, Seán Mac Réamoinn declared her first collection, *Margadh na Saoire*, the most notable book in Irish for 1956, 'ar neart na féithe aici, ar chumas na healaíon aici agus ar an máistreacht iomlán atá aici ar an dteanga Ghaeilge. Sí an mháistreacht san an tréith is sontasaí ar a saothar, dar liom' [*for the strength of her talent, her artistic ability, and complete mastery of the Irish language. That mastery is, in my view, the most notable feature of her work*]. In the *Irish Times*, John Jordan was even more effusive, declaring her ambitious long poem 'Ceathrúintí Mháire Ní Ógáin' ['Mary Hogan's Quatrains'] to be 'unquestionably the finest sequence of their kind written in Irish since the efforts to create in the revived language began [...] She is a prober of the condition of love, and no living Irish poet has brought more honesty and insight to the subject.' Seán Ó Tuama's review in *Feasta* was more sceptical. While acknowledging that there was a degree of conviction throughout the book and a fierce commitment to the native tradition, he argued that the collective voice of tradition tended to suppress her individual insight. Nonetheless, he applauded the humanity and integrity of feeling in a number of the shorter poems, identifying human relationships and the relationship with place as her primary preoccupations. Some thirty years later, in a 1984 interview, the poet herself remembered her debut collection as containing work written over almost twenty years, including 'Oíche Nollag', which she wrote at the age of fifteen, a number of school exercises, and poems devoid of inspiration, written as a way of passing the time.

The centrepiece of *Margadh na Saoire* is 'Ceathrúintí Mháire Ní Ógáin', in which the poet adopts the persona of Mary Hogan, a woman afflicted by impossible love and unable to free herself from a destructive relationship. In folk tradition, the name of Máire Ní Ógáin, who was reputedly the mistress of Donnchadh Rua Mac Con Mara, was a byword for female folly. John Jordan described the poem as an 'anatomy of passion', in which 'Crazy Jane and the Hag of Beare come together, and the resultant utterance is contemporary and timeless'. More than half a century after it was first published, the declaration of female desire in 'Ceathrúintí Mháire Ní Ógáin' maintains its transgressive force, careless of social and religious censure:

> I care little for people's suspicions,
> I care little for priests' prohibitions,
> For anything save to lie stretched
> Between you and the wall —
>
> I am indifferent to the night's cold,
> I am indifferent to the squall or rain,
> When in this warm narrow secret world
> Which does not go beyond the edge of the bed —
>
> 'MARY HOGAN'S QUATRAINS'

A generation before the groundbreaking achievements of Eavan Boland, Nuala Ní Dhomhnaill, Biddy Jenkinson, Medbh McGuckian, Eiléan Ní Chuilleanáin, Rita Ann Higgins, and others, and in more daunting social circumstances, Máire Mhac an tSaoi's poetry speaks to and from the intimate experience of women at a time when women's voices were largely inaudible, on the margins of Irish literature and society. This bilingual selection of her work is the first substantial collection to introduce her poems to an English-language audience and a reminder to readers of Irish as to why she is one of the most significant poets to emerge since the beginning of the language revival almost a century and a half ago.

THE INTEGRITY AND CANDOUR that characterise her poetry are equally evident in Máire Mhac an tSaoi's public life. Speaking of her autobiography, *The Same Age as the State* (2003), Seamus Heaney has said, 'there is truth to experience here, a forthrightness about passion and transgression that is thrilling and exemplary'. Having graduated with a degree in Modern Languages and Celtic Studies from UCD in 1942, she studied law 'without enthusiasm' and, in 1944, became the first Irish woman to be called to the bar. Awarded a Travelling Scholarship by the National University of Ireland in 1942, she spent two years (1945–7) as a graduate student in Paris, where she witnessed and shared the deprivations that followed the war. On her arrival, she and a friend were chauffeured around the city by Samuel Beckett, whom she remembers as impatient of the frivolity of his young countrywomen.

On her return from Paris in 1947, she was recruited by competitive examination to a cadetship in the Department of External Affairs, and she has spoken with characteristic frankness of her fifteen years as a civil servant and diplomat during a period of dramatic change and political turbulence in Ireland, Europe, and the developing world. She was, she says, the 'token woman' on Ireland's second delegation to the United Nations. Franco's Spain, where she served as *chargé d'affaires* at the Irish Embassy in Madrid, was 'something else again, a lethal combination of the baroque and the absurd'. She left the civil service to marry Conor Cruise O'Brien in 1962, and spent time with her husband in the Congo, Ghana, South Africa and America in dramatic times and dangerous circumstances. At a protest rally against the Vietnam War in New York, she was arrested along with Cruise O'Brien, Allen Ginsberg, and Dr Benjamin Spock. The following day the *New York Times* reported:

> The police massed more than 2,500 men yesterday and defended the induction center, a faded nine-story red brick building of 1886 construction, with barricades so formidable that Dr. Spock had to plead for an opening so that he could sit on the entrance steps and be arrested. Among those arrested were Dr. Conor Cruise O'Brien, Albert Schweitzer Professor of Humanities at New York University, and his wife Maire, daughter of the former deputy Prime Minister of Ireland, Sean MacEntee. The O'Briens were among a group staging a sit-in at Broad and Pearl Streets, one block from the induction center. Mrs. O'Brien told newsmen that mounted policemen drove their horses into the sitting group and her husband was assaulted by policemen who followed on foot. 'They [the police] kicked Conor around quite a bit,' she said. Dr. O'Brien, who headed the United Nations mission to Katanga during the 1961 Congo crisis, insisted on medical attention, according to Mrs. O'Brien. She said the police took them both to Bellevue Hospital, where it was found that Dr. O'Brien had suffered bruises. He was discharged yesterday afternoon.

> (*New York Times*, 6 December 1967)

'Mr. Ginsberg, the bearded beatnik poet', the report continued, 'was wearing an orange batik shawl, a huge flowered tie, a rosary and a Buddhist amulet. There were cymbals on his fingers, of the sort affected by Egyptian belly dancers, and he made a cheerful tinkle as the police hustled him to a van'. Decades after the event, the poet recalled with considerable amusement a telegram received by her husband from a friend after their arrest: 'Hear you got kicked by a cop.

What was his ethnicity?' While that particular incident passed off without violence, according to the *New York Times*, her autobiography records more lethal encounters. One of the most powerful passages in *The Same Age as the State* recounts an apparent attempt to assassinate Dr O'Brien in Katanga.

M ÁIRE MHAC AN TSAOI is one of a trinity of poets who revolutionised Irish language poetry in the 1940s and 50s. While their collective achievements mark the high-point of modernist poetry in Irish, each has a distinctive, and defining, relationship with the language and its literary traditions. Seán Ó Ríordáin's poetic voice derives its particular accent from the struggle with a 'language that is half-mine' and the unresolved conflict with a tradition he finds necessary but suffocating, while Máirtín Ó Direáin draws confidently on the resources of the spoken language of Aran and a literary tradition he accepts as a legitimate cultural inheritance. The work of Dublin-born Máire Mhac an tSaoi is marked by greater deference to Gaeltacht tradition than either Ó Direáin, born and raised in the Irish-speaking community of Inis Mór, or Ó Ríordáin, who spent his formative years in the bilingual breac-Ghaeltacht of Baile Bhuirne.

That her relationship with the oral and literary traditions of the Munster Gaeltacht of Corca Dhuibhne is a hallmark of her work is acknowledged by critics of her work from the outset. As in the case of the great Scots-Gaelic poet Somhairle Mac Gill-Eain, the depth of her knowledge of tradition and the intensity of her engagement with its established procedures owe a great deal to her personal circumstances and upbringing in a family steeped in the Irish language and its literary heritage. While she protests that indolence caused her to abandon her ambition to be an actress or a teacher, her scholarly work on classical Irish of the twelfth to the seventeenth century was a vindication of her mother's enthusiasm for the linguistic and intellectual virtuosity of early modern poetry in Irish. Students who attended her mother's lectures on classical Irish love poetry at UCD will remember, the poet tells us in *The Same Age as the State*, 'the extraordinary phenomenon of a warm and witty twentieth-century, middle-aged, middle-class Irish lady entering completely into the mind of the medieval Gaelic poet in his lighter moments, and communicating her understanding and her enjoyment to her hearers'. She acknowledges that her own imagination was full of echoes of early modern syllabic poetry and the more popular folk love songs when she began to write in her mid-teens. Maternal influence in that regard was further extended by that of her uncle Monsignor Pádraig de Brún, translator of Homer, Danté, Racine, and Sophocles into Irish, and one of the most distinguished literary figures of his time. A mathematician by training, and a former student of Eamon de Valera, Mgr de Brún served as President of University College Galway from 1945 to 1959. His friend Thomas MacGreevy referred to him as 'Rector Magnificus', and spoke of his 'Olympian capacity to appreciate the most exalted works of art and literature, ancient and modern'.

Deeply affected by the execution of the leaders of the 1916 rising, and particularly of his close friend Seán MacDermott, Mgr de Brún built a home in Dún Chaoin, where his sister's children spent up to five months a year from the age of two so that, the poet says, she can never remember a time when she was not bilingual. Tigh na Cille served as a kind of vernacular university where her uncle held court among his cultural and intellectual peers, local masters of the native poetic tradition, masters also of the art of poetic speech, as she recalls in a late poem:

> Discerning neighbours, adept with oar and spade,
> And in no way at a loss on the paths of learning —
> Did they not teach you how
> To transform your learning into the beauty of their native Irish? —
> They were giants whose descendants turned out to be dwarfs!

'Not Forgotten: Disparaged'

That the miraculous parish of Dún Chaoin left a permanent mark on the emerging poet's imagination is evident from the concluding verses of one of her earliest poems, 'Slán', translated here by Douglas Sealy:

> It's not on the dreary streets of Dublin,
> Though its people see me as one of their own,
> That my scattered thoughts go their wandering way
> In the dark and lonesome stretches of the night.
>
> They go their way to the far western seaboard
> Where the sun goes down in the yellow glory of evening,
> A land of hills and coves, of isles and inlets,
> The only place in the world where my heart is free.
>
> 'FAREWELL'

The rejection of the contemporary suburban world of her native Dublin in favour of a poetic territory that is as much an imagined as it is a physical location is one of the more confronting aspects of Máire Mhac an tSaoi's work for many readers. It is both fundamental to her poetics and, as we shall see, incomplete. While there is clearly an element of romanticism in her construction of the Gaeltacht, her reverence for this Dún Chaoin of memory and imagination derives less from a sense that the idyllic world of childhood is on the brink of disappearance, than from a profound feeling that the language and community to which she gained access in her early years was more substantial, more meaningful, than the culturally fragmented, uncertain world of post-revolutionary English-speaking Ireland. In an article published in the poetry journal *Innti* in 1988, she insisted that, as a child, this Gaeltacht world seemed to her impervious to time, classical, preordained, whole:

Mhaireas os cionn leathchéad bliain ins an chluthaireacht san,
á iompar timpeall liom im intinn go dtí gur dhúisíos ó chianai-
bhín agus go bhfuaireas mo chruinne ché leata ar an aer agus
ceiliúrtha. Tá sé ródhéanach agam malairt timpeallachta a ch-
uardach. Deirtí go mba phioróid é an cainteoir dúchais deire-
annach a mhair de chuid Bhreatain Chorn, agus gur chónaigh
sé i Ringsend. Mise an phioróid sin.

[*I lived in that warmth for more than fifty years, carrying it around
with me in my head until I woke a short while ago and found my world
scattered to the wind, dispersed. It is too late for me to look for another
habitat. It used to be said that that the last native speaker of Cornish
was a parrot and that he lived in Ringsend. I am that parrot.*]

That the geography of her imagination no longer corresponds to a
physical, or, indeed, a linguistic reality, hardly lessens the validity or
the intensity of her poetic insight. It might even be argued that the
counterfactuality of her poetic universe heightens its effect, adding
to its poignancy.

I F THE IRISH OF DÚN CHAOIN provided her with a poetic me-
dium, rooted in the vernacular *caint na ndaoine* and endorsed by
generations of aristocratic and popular poets, there are other
reasons why the literary tradition of the West Kerry Gaeltacht was
conducive to a young poet determined to explore the more intimate
aspects of female experience in an Ireland where such intimacy re-
mained largely unspoken. The Irish language provided her with pow-
erful precedents for the forthright expression of female desire, in
the older literary tradition and in the anonymous voices that speak
in the great love songs of the oral tradition. All of these are present
as enabling exemplars in Máire Mhac an tSaoi's early work, provid-
ing outspoken models of the feminine, sanctioned by tradition, and
a radical alternative to the circumscribed femininity of Ireland in the
1940s and 50s. In early Irish literature, aristocratic women such as

Deirdre and Gráinne appear careless of the disastrous consequences of unfettered desire, maintaining their emotional independence despite the restrictions of social and moral convention. While conservative supporters viewed the Irish language as a kind of cultural innoculation against vice, 'a general national prophylactic', according to Myles na gCopaleen, the sexual behaviour of some of the most illustrious figures in early Irish literature and mythology is clearly at odds with the moral values of mid-twentieth-century Ireland. In the later song tradition, sexuality is celebrated without shame or embarrassment while the frustration of unrequited love and unconsummated passion is reprehensible, the ultimate betrayal. In poems such as 'AthDheirdre', 'Suantraí Ghráinne', 'Freagra', 'An seanaghalar', 'Ceathrúintí Mháire Ní Ógáin', and 'Iníon a' Lóndraigh', Máire Mhac an tSaoi draws on the resources of the native tradition to articulate aspects of female sexuality that are subversive of orthodox morality, transgressing knowingly against the prevailing values of the time and place in which they were written. In other poems, such as 'Cad is bean?' and 'A fhir dar fhulaingeas', she invokes the anti-romantic aspects of the native tradition to explore the more destructive elements of relationships between men and women. In conversation, she likes to quote a contemporary of hers in Dunquin saying, of a made match, 'Fanadh sé leis féin, an stail!' [*Let him stay on his own, the stallion!*].

T HE EXTENT TO WHICH Máire Mhac an tSaoi's individual poetic voice is strengthened or submerged by her deference to tradition has been the subject of much comment by critics. In her early love poems, she has chosen, for the most part, not to speak in the voice of a contemporary middle-class Dublin woman, but rather through the reconstructed voices of female characters from early Irish literature and the oral song tradition. While her poetic method reduces her weaker poems to the level of pastiche, her imitation of the conventions of traditional verse in Irish is more than an act of homage, it is an enabling strategy that permits the expression of the otherwise inexpressible. The authority of distinguished literary precedent provides both a decoy and an alibi for the indirect, but nonetheless forthright, articulation of transgressive experience:

> The child of jealousy is sucking my breast,
> While I nurse it day and night;
> The ugly brat is cutting teeth,
> My veins throb with the venom of its bite.
>
> My love, may the little wretch not remain between us,
> Seeing how healthy and full was our knowledge of each other;
> It was a skin warranty that kept us together,
> And a seal of hand that knew no bounds.

'MARY HOGAN'S QUATRAINS'

In an interview with Harry Kreisler in 2000, the poet identified 'refusal' as her principal theme. The dramatic lyrics, which are her preferred poetic mode, grew out of 'abortive love affairs of my own', deriving their structure from a refusal of commitment, a determination to withdraw from impending crisis: 'In most of my poetry you can see that drawing back, bringing the poem right up to the crisis, and pulling back; elegantly, of course'. In an earlier conversation with Michael Davitt, published in 1984, she indicated that the love poems in her first collection were drawn from actual experience but that the context had been altered: 'Tá daoine agus mothú ar leithligh i gceist sna dánta grá agus ní gá go mbeadh an timpeallacht díreach de réir mar a tharla. Tá finscéalaíocht sa timpeallacht in a lán acu' [*There are specific people and feelings involved in the love poems and the context does not necessarily correspond to what actually happened. The folkloric provides a context in many of them*]. While there may be sound personal reasons for the technique of simultaneous discretion and disclosure practised under the cloak and mask of tradition, the poet also provided an alternative explanation for this aspect of her work, arguing that the dramatic lyric is, in any event, the principle mode of Irish poetry: 'De ghnáth ní labhrann file Éireannach mar gheall air féin ach amháin i bpearsa choinbhinsiúnta. Deineann sé neamhphearsanú air féin. Fiú amháin Aodhagán Ó Rathaille, nuair a chloiseann tú an glór mór pearsanta ag gabháil tríd, is toisc go bhfuil cuing na neamhphearsantachta air atá sé chomh láidir san. Labhrann sé ar son na treibhe' [*The Irish poet speaks only through a conventional persona for the most part. He depersonalises the self. Even Aodhagán Ó Rathaille, when you hear that powerful personal voice in his work, a large part of its impact derives from the strictures of the impersonal. He speaks for the tribe*]. In this she is at one with scholars who have identified the dramatic lyric as the dominant mode of poetic composition in Irish, from the poems attributed to Colmcille, St Patrick, Oisín, Liadan, and the Hag of Beare, to the anonymous female voices that speak in 'Dónal Óg', 'Liam Ó Raghallaigh' and the great songpoems that survive in the living tradition of *sean-nós* singing. For a poet immersed in the native tradition, the dramatic lyric provides a poetic form, sanctioned by authoritative precedents, for the expression of intense emotions that transgress the established moral code of her own time and place. It also provides a necessary distance for a poet who insists that she only writes under extraordinary emotional pressure, a structure that facilitates the exploration and articulation of traumatic experience that might otherwise remain inchoate and silent. For her audience in the 1940s and 50s, a suitable distance may also have been necessary. It is difficult to imagine poems such as 'Ceathrúintí Mháire Ní Ógáin' escaping censure, or, indeed, censorship, if female desire were to be expressed with equal candour in the voice of a contemporary, suburban Dublin woman.

MÁIRE MHAC AN TSAOI CONTINUED writing and publishing poems in Irish and English until, she says in her 1988 essay, 'Dhá arm aigne', reading Lorca during her posting at the Irish embassy in Madrid persuaded her to abandon English in the late 1940s. The folk elements in his *Romancero Gitano*, reminiscent of the Irish-language tradition and its tendency to surrealism, persuaded her to commit herself finally to Irish as the sole medium of poetic expression. Her Irish, she realised, had the authority necessary for poetry while her 'secondary school English' had neither colour nor conviction: 'Ní raibh an bhuntsraith éachtach tuaithe agam a bhí ag mo mháthair agus ag na huncailí, agus ní raghadh Béarla léannta na hochtú aoise déag, a bhí fós beo in ár dteaghlach, abhaile ar an lucht léite ar a raibh mo shúil' [*I didn't have the extraordinary underlay of rural English that my mother and uncles had, and the more learned eighteenth-century English, that was still current in our family, would not have the necessary impact on the audience I sought*]. She lacked, she says, the ability to integrate the available registers of English to develop an adequate poetic dialect in English of the kind that Berryman, for instance, had achieved in America.

While Lorca may well have been a catalyst for her subsequent work, he also provided a retrospective validation of tendencies already evident in her earliest poems. By the time she completed her first translation of Lorca, 'An bhean mhídhílis', in 1951, she had written all of the other poems included in *Margadh na Saoire*, her first and most substantial collection. Despite the difference in location, the adulterous assignation among the bonfires in Lorca's 'La casada infiel', the final poem in the book, is thematically consistent with the rain-drenched encounter of the earlier 'Ceathrúintí Mháire Ní Ógáin'. While commentators have rightly drawn attention to the European dimension of her work, there is no contradiction between this international frame of reference and her commitment to the native Irish tradition, a tradition heavily inflected throughout its history by classical and European influence. The tradition within which she has chosen to locate the *terroir* of her imagination is neither insular nor provincial, but confident, as she is, of its ability to integrate external influences. Translating Rilke, Shakespeare, Lorca, and others, has been largely a pastime, she says, a substitute for original work when inspiration was absent, and, crucially, a way of maintaining her facility with Irish during extended absences from direct contact with the spoken dialect of Corca Dhuibhne.

I F THE MORE HIGHLY WROUGHT, elaborate poems are the most immediately compelling aspects of Máire Mhac an tSaoi's work, Seán Ó Tuama has drawn attention to the gentler tone of others that celebrate less fraught intimacies. 'One can see, however, in her best lyrics, lyrics that are often concerned with moments of love and companionship, that her passionate sensibility is most evident when she restrains her remarkable eloquence, cuts back on traditional flourishes' (1991). The more relaxed style and subdued language of early poems of friendship such as 'Do Shíle', and 'Comhrá ar shráid', give the impression of being closer to the actual details of lived experience. The same might be said of 'An chéad bhróg', also from her first collection, which places the apparently ordinary occasion of a child being fitted for his first pair of shoes at the centre of a poetic universe. These, and poems of maternal solicitude such as 'Máiréad sa tsiopa cóirithe gruaige', and 'Codladh an ghaiscígh', represent a reordering of the thematics of poetry similar to Eavan Boland's *Nightfeed* (1982) where a mother feeding her child in a suburban kitchen is an occasion of utmost significance.

> Five years old! My amber flower!
> It was foolish of me to fix your hair
> So lightly you stepped to the hairdresser
> To be soaped and scissored, pinned and dried
> With such good grace, willing and obliging
> As a lamb to its raddle for shearing and marking
> Until you landed on earth like Shirley Temple,
> Though not so pale, a charming girl,
> Before the mirror revealed the new you ... and then
> Oh such lamentation may I never hear again!
> With your head in my lap you wept your fill —
> I won't pretend I don't know what horrified you:
> Love, marriage, the monthly blood all
> Staring back, childbearing, the common lot.
> Bless your little head and your crowning glory
> As you bawl your eyes out at your mother's waist

With hatred for the female and no escape from it!
My soul's treasure, if only I could help you I would.

'Margaret in the Hairdressers'

While these alternative modes are more frequently deployed in her later work, they are present from the outset. The poet herself has identified 'Do Shíle', one of the earliest compositions in her debut collection, as the first poem in which she managed to express something of the actual circumstances of her life satisfactorily in a modern context, without recourse to the folkloric. As her circumstances changed, with marriage and the arrival of children, she says, more of the actual details of her life as a suburban wife and mother began to infiltrate the poems, which became more securely anchored to the present tense and the quotidian. 'Tán tú ceangailte insa lá atá inniu ann nuair atá clann agat' [*You are entangled in the present when you have children*] (2010). She has also said that the advent of children provoked a return to writing after an extended period of silence.

This is not to suggest that the later poems are somehow more authentic in their engagement with experience, but that there is a change of emphasis in both subject matter and style as Shirley Temple replaces Máire Ní Ógáin, and friends and family members are named side by side with Cúchulainn and Pierce Ferriter's Iníon a' Lóndraigh. The ghost of Eoghan Rua Ó Súilleabháin is summoned by an impertinent schoolgirl in 'Maireann an tseanamhuintir', while street children beg on a city bridge and the neighbour's children infect her son with headlice in 'Gníomhartha corpartha na trócaire'. Again, while the presence of actual women she has known is a more prominent feature of the later work, their arrival centre stage is anticipated in her earliest poems where Sheila May, the dedicatee of 'Do Shíle', the anonymous Kerryman in 'Comhrá ar shráid', and Olga Popovic, the Frenchwoman who provides a model of fearless independence in 'Gan réiteach', are among the *dramatis personae* alongside the heroes of literature, folklore, and mythology.

In 1989 Seán Mac Réamoinn argued that there is no discernible development through distinct phases in Máire Mhac an tSaoi's work, but that her technique is sufficiently flexible to allow for considerable variation in theme and tone while maintaining consistency of style. It is a valid point as one of her most celebrated poems from the 1973 collection of the same name, 'Codladh an Ghaiscígh', draws on a broad range of sources in the literary and oral traditions of the Gaeltacht to express a mother's delight in the prowess of her young son, while also addressing her husband by name and speaking directly of the boy's adoption from a country where 'never trust the white is the prayer of your people by right'. It is a poem as securely anchored in the native tradition as the imitations of literary and folk exemplars among her earliest apprentice pieces and as contemporary as the most achieved of her later work in its exploration of the actual circumstances of her own experience as a mother and wife. While the later elegies for dead friends and family use the conventions of traditional lament, they still convey the specificity of each particular grief and the individual personality of the deceased:

> Your angers are at rest, and your pitiful body
> Rots in the grave;
> But you'll be my companion tonight
> And all the rest of my days:
> Two females alive in their imagination,
> Turning into grass,
> No limits to their eloquence
> And no fear of the clergy —
> I swear to God!
>
> 'A New Edge on an Old Saw'

Here again, it is the integration of traditional formulae with the tones and textures of her own poetic voice, and the careful calibration of language appropriate to the moment and occasion of each poem, that characterise her best work.

M OST CRITICISM OF Máire Mhac an tSaoi's work provides a reprise of the notes sounded by her first reviewers. Her champions applaud her uncompromising exploration of the feminine and her confident manipulation of language and form, while her detractors charge her with excessive devotion to dialect and convention as a retreat from the actual, leading ultimately to artificiality and inauthenticity. Mac Réamoinn has provided the most persuasive defense of her poetic method, reminding readers that technical experiment, including imitation of traditional forms, is a necessary prelude to innovation and a legitimate demonstration of the ludic dimension of the literary imagination. Her engagement with her literary inheritance is, he argues, a precondition for the emergence of a distinctive poetic voice buttressed by tradition, strengthened rather than suppressed by established conventions of language and form. Her style is her own, he says, the poetic diction inherited from the dead generations. He provides a further refinement of her sense of place by pointing out that her territorial affiliation is local rather than national. 'Níor mhiste a rá, bíodh go bhfuil breis agus *petite patrie* amháin aici, nach léir aon cheangal *le grande patrie*, ná dílseacht dá leithéid' [*It may be worth mentioning that although she has more than one petite patrie there is little evidence of any affiliation or loyalty to any grande patrie*]. Two poems in the present volume, 'Cam reilige 1916-1966' and 'Fód an imris: Ard-Oifig an Phoist 1986', addressed to her father Seán MacEntee, who fought in the GPO in 1916 and on the republican side in the Civil War, subsequently serving in De Valera's government as Minister for Finance and Tánaiste, might be read as an oblique critique of militant Irish nationalism.

Having reiterated Ó Tuama's identification of the relationship with place and with others as her central preoccupations, Mac Réamoinn extends the list to include her exploration of the relationship with herself. Ultimately, it is the unflinching confrontation with the self at moments of crisis and revelation that generates her most accomplished poems. Although her work has been less than prolific, she has continued to explore the particularities of the female experience, both positive and negative, from the first awakening of sexuality to the decline of old age and the death of loved ones. Micheál Ó Siadhail has observed that her poems are so comprehensive of the female experience, so saturated with the feminine that the feminine becomes a model of the human: 'Tá an oiread banúlacht ina cuid dánta gur duiniúlacht uilig ar deireadh iad' [*There is so much of the feminine in them that ultimately they are all humanity*].

Máire Mhac an tSaoi's influence on subsequent generations of women poets, in Irish and in English, has been significant and enduring. It is particularly strong among the Irish-language poets who emerged in the 1970s and 80s to further extend the revolution in poetics she had initiated thirty years earlier. While the strength of women's voices in contemporary poetry clearly owes a great deal to the social revolution of the women's movement, the presence of a powerful female antecedent has been cited by Nuala Ní Dhomhnaill, Biddy Jenkinson and others as crucial in the discovery and development of their own poetic voices. For Ní Dhomhnaill and Jenkinson, the oral and literary dimensions of the Irish-language tradition are enabling rather than disabling precedents, capable of apparently endlessly productive reconfiguration in a contemporary setting. In this they are indebted to Máire Mhac an tSaoi, whose own distinctive voice is now an integral part of that shared inheritance.

THIS BILINGUAL VOLUME includes poems from all of Máire Mhac an tSaoi's five collections in Irish, *Margadh na Saoire* (1956), *Codladh an Ghaiscígh* (1973), *An Galar Dubhach* (1980), *An Cion go dtí Seo* (1987) and *Shoa agus Dánta Eile* (1999) and a number of uncollected recent poems. The selection was made from a provisional list drawn up by the editor, with subsequent inclusions and exclusions made on the advice of individual translators and of the poet herself. The final selection was made by the editor and the author. The translators have worked directly from the Irish to provide English translations that remain close to the originals, while attempting to provide a parallel in English that matches, as far as possible, the different tone and temper of each individual poem. While an attempt has been made in some instances to replicate the form of the original, the translations are more concerned with precision in vocabulary and imagery, and with matching the inflections of Máire Mhac an tSaoi's voice which vary from one poem to the next. It should be possible for a diligent reader to move from the Irish poem to the English translation and back again without feeling that (s)he had been wrongfooted, or deliberately misled.

The courage and scruple that have marked Máire Mhac an tSaoi's life and work have been demonstrated again in her generous collaboration on this project. That her poetic imagination remains alive and responsive to the passing moment is evident in the poems she has produced while the book was being compiled. 'Nec patris linquens dexteram', 'Máiréad', 'Mo chumha', and 'Ceann bliana', written for her husband Conor a year after his death, are reminiscent of Old Irish poetry in their brevity and uncluttered simplicity. It might even be argued that the clarity and integrity of these late poems represent the culmination of a lifelong commitment to language, form, and truth, as poetic utterance appears a pure distillation of experience, discarding all inessentials to bridge the gap between word and world:

> I arrange my memory in readiness for the grave,
> Put spices in her shroud and silver coins;
> The snow is still on the cemetery ridge;
> I lie down beside the body on my bed.

'A YEAR LATER'

LOUIS DE PAOR
Ionad an Léinn Éireannaigh
Ollscoil na hÉireann, Gaillimh

Bigart, Homer. '264 seized here in draft protest', *The New York Times*, 6 December 1967.

Ó Corcora, Dónall. 'Dán cruinn beo', *Feasta*, Feabhra 1953, 16–17.

Cronin, Anthony. *No Laughing Matter: The Life and Times of Flann O'Brien* (London: Paladin Books 1990), 136.

Cruise O'Brien, Máire. *The Same Age as the State* (Dublin: O'Brien Press 2003).

Heaney, Seamus. Quoted on front cover of paperback edition of *The Same Age as the State*.

Jordan, John. 'A native poet', *The Irish Times*, 23 February 1957.

Mac Réamoinn, Seán. 'Leabhra na Nollag', *Comhar*, Nollaig 1956, 26–7.

Mac Réamoinn. 'Athnuachan an traidisiúin', *Comhar*, Eanáir 1989, 22–6.

MacGreevy, Thomas. 'Tribute to the late Monsignor Pádraig de Brún', *The Capuchin Annual*, Dublin 1961, 371–2, (MacGreevy Archive).

Mhac an tSaoi, Máire. In conversation with Michael Davitt, 'Mo dhiachair áilleacht bhristechroíoch', *Innti* 8, 1984, 38–59.

Mhac an tSaoi. 'Dhá arm aigne', *Innti* 11, 1988, 14–15.

Mhac an tSaoi. In conversation with Harry Kreisler, University of California, Berkeley, 4 April 2000, 'Conversations with history: Irish poetry, Maire MacEntee', http://conversations.berkeley.edu/content/maire-macentee.

Mhac an tSaoi. In conversation with Louis de Paor, Beann Éadair, 4 September 2010.

Ó Siadhail, Micheál. 'Cheithre bliana fichead de ród', *Comhar*, Márta 1981, 30.

Ó Tuama, Seán. 'Saothar teann tíorthúil', *Feasta*, Márta 1957, 14–16.

Ó Tuama. 'Twentieth century poetry in Irish', *Krino* 11, 1991, 26–31.

AN PARÓISTE MÍORÚILTEACH

THE MIRACULOUS PARISH

ROGHA DÁNTA **SELECTED POEMS**

Oíche Nollag

Le coinnle na n-aingeal tá an spéir amuigh breactha,
Tá fiacail an tseaca sa ghaoith ón gcnoc,
Adaigh an tine is téir chun na leapan,
Luífidh Mac Dé ins an tigh seo anocht.

Fágaig' an doras ar leathadh ina coinne,
An mhaighdean a thiocfaidh is a naí ar a hucht,
Deonaigh scíth an bhóthair a ligint, a Mhuire,
Luíodh Mac Dé ins an tigh seo anocht.

Bhí soilse ar lasadh i dtigh sin na haíochta,
Cóiriú gan caoile, bia agus deoch,
Do cheannaithe olla, do cheannaithe síoda,
Ach luífidh Mac Dé ins an tigh seo anocht.

Christmas Eve

With candles of angels the sky is now dappled,
The frost on the wind from the hills has a bite,
Kindle the fire and go to your slumber,
Jesus will lie in this household tonight.

Leave all the doors wide open before her,
The Virgin who'll come with the child on her breast,
Grant that you'll stop here tonight, Holy Mary,
That Jesus a while in this household may rest.

The lights were all lighting in that little hostel,
There were generous servings of victuals and wine,
For merchants of silk, for merchants of woollens,
But Jesus will lie in this household tonight.

(GF)

Do Shíle

Cuimhním ar sheomra ó thaobh na farraige,
Aniar is aneas do bheireadh scríb air,
Is báisteach ar fhuinneoig ina clagarnaigh,
Gan sánas air ó thitim oíche,
Is is cuimhin liom go rabhais ann, a Shíle,
Suite go híseal cois na tine
Is an fáinne óir ar do mhéir linbh.

Do thugais dúinn amhrán croíbhuartha,
Is ba cheol na fliúite le clos do ghlór ann,
Comharthaí grá ón bhFrainc ar cuairt chughainn —
Bhí gile do chinn mar an t-airgead luachra
Fé sholas an lampa leagtha ar bord ann.

Nach cuma feasta, a naí bhig, eadrainn
Deighilt na mblianta nó fuatha an charadais?
Dob é mo dhán an tráth san t'aithne.

For Sheila

I remember a room on the seaward side —
The squall caught it from the south-west —
And rain a tattoo on the window
Unslackening since the fall of night,
And I remember that you were there, Sheila,
Sitting low by the fire,
The gold ring on your childlike finger.

You gave us a heartbroken song
And your voice was the music of flutes,
Love's catalogue brought here from France —
The fairness of your head was like the meadowsweet
Under the light of the lamp set on the table.

What do they matter more, little dear one, between us,
Separation of years, and aversions bred of friendship?
It was my lot to know you at that time.

(vi)

Comhrá ar shráid

Ar leacacha na sráide
Nuair tharla ort an lá san
Do labhrais chugham chomh tláith sin
Am fhiafraí go muinteartha
Gur bhog an t-aer im thimpeall,
Aer bocht leamh na cathrach,
Le leoithne bhog aniar chughainn
Ó dhúthaigh cois farraige
Inar chuireas ort aithne…

An tsiúráil réidh sin,
Fios do bhéasa féin agat,
Teann as do Ghaelainn,
As do dheisbhéalaí
Mhín chúirtéisigh —
Ní leanbh ó aréir mé,
A Chiarraígh shéimh sin,
Ach creid mé gur fhéadais
Mé a chur ó bhuíochas
Mo dhaoine féinig.

Street-Talk

On the flagged street
That day we happened to meet
You spoke to me so kindly
Asking courteously how I was,
That the air softened around me,
The dull impoverished city air,
With a little breeze you brought
From the west, from that place
By the sea where I first knew you…

That easy confidence,
And knowing how to behave,
Certain of your language,
Your gentle wit and
Courtly ability with it —
I was not born yesterday,
My gracious Kerry friend,
But believe me you could have
Turned me away from
My nearest and dearest.

(LP)

AthDheirdre

'Ní bhearrfad m'ingne',
Adúirt sí siúd
Is do thug cúl don saol
De dheascaibh an aonlae sin —
Lena cré
Ní mhaífinnse,
Ná mo leithéidse, gaol —
Cíoraim mo cheann
Is cuirim dath fém béal.

No Second Deirdre

'I will not pare my nails',
She said
And turned her back on the world
For the sake of that solitary day —
With her breed
Neither I nor my likes
Would claim affinity —
        I comb my hair
        And colour my lips.

(LP)

Jack

Strapaire fionn sé troithe ar airde,
Mac feirmeora ó iarthar tíre
Ná cuimhneoidh feasta go rabhas-sa oíche
Ar urlár suimint' aige ag rince.

Ach ní dhearúdfad a ghéaga im thimpeall,
A gháire ciúin ná a chaint shibhialta —
Ina léine bhán, is a ghruaig nuachíortha
Buí fén lampa ar bheagán íle …

Fágfaidh a athair talamh ina dhiaidh aige,
Pósfaidh bean agus tógfaidh síolbhach,
Ach mar chonacthas domhsa é arís ní cífear,
Beagbheann ar chách ób' gheal lem chroí é.

Barr dá réir go raibh air choíche!
Rath is séan san áit ina mbíonn sé!
Mar atá tréitheach go dté crích air —
Dob é an samhradh so mo rogha 'pháirtí é.

Jack

A fine fair-headed six-foot fellow,
A farmer's son from the country westward,
On hard cement we danced together
A night in the future he'll not remember,

But I won't forget how his arms embraced me
His quiet smile, civil conversation —
In his clean white shirt, his neat combed hair —
Yellow in the lamplight as the oil ran lower.

He'll get the land his father leaves him,
Marry and raise a houseful of children
But no-one will see the man I danced with —
What did I care who saw my fancy.

All that is best in the world I wish him,
Blessings on every place that holds him,
Every promise fulfilled in living,
My chosen partner for all this summer.

(EC)

Finit

Le seans a chuala uathu scéala an chleamhnais
Is b'ait liom srian le héadroime na gaoithe —
Do bhís chomh hanamúil léi, chomh domheabhartha,
Chomh fiáin léi, is chomh haonraic, mar ba chuimhin liom.

Féach feasta go bhfuil dála cháich i ndán duit,
Cruatan is coitinne, séasúr go céile,
Ag éalú i ndearúd le hiompú ráithe
Gur dabht arbh ann duit riamh, ná dod leithéidse...

Ach go mbeidh poirt anois ná cloisfead choíche
Gan tú bheith os mo chomhair arís sa chúinne
Ag feitheamh, ceol ar láimh leat, roimh an rince
Is diamhaireacht na hoíche amuigh id shúile.

Finit

By chance I heard them mention
Your engagement. The wind died down,
Grew tame. You were the wind — wilful,
Spirited, as I remember. Untamed. Solitary.

Henceforth, know the common lot
Is yours, hardship and routine, season
By season, slipping from memory as the quarters turn
Till we doubt that you or your like ever existed.

But there will be tunes I'll never hear again
Without seeing you there in the corner,
Melodeon in hand, waiting for the dance,
Your eyes, the darkness of the night, brought in.

(BJ)

Freagra

'Ná tabhair chun seanabhróga é mar ghrá —
Éirímis as, anois an t-am againn:
Grá bocht díomhaoin nár ghabh riamh thar chomhrá,
Nár theann go tráth na bpóg, grá scanraithe
A dhiúltaigh roimh admháil. Ná mealltar sinn
Fé ghrian aon pheata lae; ní fiú an barr
Fionraí go teacht an fhómhair — Ó cabhraigh liom!
Do shroich an phréamh an croí is do chuaigh go lár!'

'Och, a mhaoinín, ná goil, ná goil go fóill —
Luigh leis an áthas atá anois féd réir.
Ná santaigh síoreiteach is síoréaló,
Ná féach chun cinn ach glac gach ní ina chéim,
Sólás nó pian go humhal ó ló go ló…
            Ní briseadh croí is dán do gach aon spéir.'

Reply

'Why wait till love dies?
Give up, give in. It's time.
Poor languid love that never crossed the line
Of conversation, never reached the kiss. Petrified
Love, denied admission. One pet day
Should not seduce us. Such a small harvest.
Why delay the reaping? — And yet so help me!
The root has reached the heart and taken hold.'

'Don't cry awhile, dear heart, don't cry —
Lie with the joy you have.
Don't always seek rejection and escape.
Don't look ahead but take things in their stride
Solace and sorrow take in equal share.
Go humbly, day by day.
          Not every dawn is doomed to break a heart.'

(BJ)

Inquisitio 1584

Sa bhliain sin d'aois Ár dTiarna
Chúig chéad déag cheithre fichid,
Nó blianta beaga ina dhiaidh sin,
Seán mac Éamoinn mhic Uilig
Lámh le Sionainn do crochadh —

Lámh le Sionainn na scuainte
I Luimnigh, cathair na staire,
Seán mac Éamoinn mhic Uilig
Aniar ó pharóiste Mhárthain,
Ba thaoiseach ar Bhaile an Fhianaigh.

Tréas an choir, is a thailte
Do tugadh ar láimh strainséara;
Is anois fé bhun Chruach Mhárthain
Níl cuimhne féin ar a ainm,
Fiú cérbha díobh ní feasach ann…

Nára corrach do shuan,
A Sheáin mhic Éamoinn mhic Uilig,
Ar bhruach na Sionainne móire
Nuair 'shéideann gaoth ón bhfarraige
Aniar ód cheantar dúchais.

Inquisitio 1584

In the year of Our Lord
Fifteen hundred and eighty four
Or a year or two thereafter
Seán mac Éamoinn mhic Uilig
By the Shannon water they hanged —

By the teeming Shannon water
In Limerick's storied city
Seán mac Éamoinn mhic Uilig
From the westerly parish of Márthain
Who was chieftain of Baile an Fhianaigh.

Treason the crime, and his lands
Gifted to a stranger's hands.
Now beneath the Hill of Márthain
Not even his name is remembered
Or who his people were.

May your sleep be not troubled
Seán mac Éamoinn mhic Uilig
On the bank of the great Shannon
When the wind from the sea blows
Eastward from your native place.

(PS)

Ar an mórshlua

'Daoine sona an méid nach mair' —
File i ngrá gan gruaim á rá;
Cé dhó is fearr is fios anois?
Fada fé bhrat talún atá.

The Way of All Flesh

'Happy the dead.'
So said the poet,
Easily: he was in love.
Now he knows if it is so.
Over him, grass grows.

(BJ)

Gan réiteach

'Ní heolach dom cad é, eagla an bháis,'
Is nuair a labhair do chuala na trompaí
Is chonac an pobal fiáin is an fhuil sa tsráid,
Is do bhí lasair thóirse agus gaoith
Fé na bratacha i gcaint an Fhrancaigh mhná.

Is do scanraíos, a dheoranta is a bhí,
Gur deacair liom scarúint le teas ón ngréin;
'Mo chreach!' adúrt, 'is fada ins an chill
Don gcolainn is is uaigneach sa chré' —
      Ach d'iompaigh sí a súile móra orm,
      Lán de mhíthuiscint uaibhrigh, is níor ghéill.

Intractable

'Fear of death, what's that?'
And at the words I heard the trumpets sound,
Saw frenzied crowds, blood on the streets.
A torch flamed and the wind shook out the flags
In the Frenchwoman's speech.

I startled. Alien to me
To turn from the sun's warmth;
'Alas!' I said, 'The body spends a long time in the grave
And it is lonesome there' —
   She looked at me, eyes blind with arrogance
   And didn't yield.

(BJ)

Feabhra

Le dhá lá nó le trí do bhog an uain,
Do ghabhas an t-aer mar fhallaing ar mo chorp—
Milis, a Dhé, rómhilis an séasúr!
Leachta gach cruaidh; ní buan ann oighear ná toil.

Dall agus bodhar, a dhaoine romham sa tslí,
Ná cífidh an t-earrach ghabh t, a dhaoine romham sa tslí,
Ná cífidh an t-earrach ghabh tríom ina cheatha
Sciúrtha mar phrás a nitear, ná hairíonn
San aer im thimpeall tinneall sreanga teanna.

Aibigh, a mhian, i ndiamhaireacht na gile,
Ar bior le tuiscint aonraic ar an ndúil;
I gcoim na mire fite mar a bhfuilir
Dulta ó aithint súl, bí teann, a rún.

February

The weather softened in the last few days.
I took the air for raiment.
Sweet, Jesus, honey sweet the season!
Rocks melt. Nor ice nor reason hold.

You're blind and deaf, you people who pass by
And will not see spring pierce me with bright showers
Of gleaming brass, and will not hear
Around me, quivering strings.

Quicken, love, in darknesses of light,
Sharp with desire,
Delirious, and out of ken of kin,
Stand firm, my soul, hold tight.

(BJ)

An chéad bhróg

d'Eoin Dáibhí

Do chuireamar an bhróg air den gcéad uair ar maidin,
Fáiscithe, fuaite, seoidín den leathar,
Míorúilt ghréasaíochta sa chéadscoth den bhfaisean
Ar an dtroigh bheag bhláfar nár chaith cuing cheana,
An chéad bhróg riamh ar an gcoisín meala.

A mhaoinín, a chroí istigh, seo leat ag satailt,
Buail an bonn nó so go teann ar an dtalamh,
Tóg an ceann gleoite go clóchasach, daingean,
Linbhín fir tú id shiúl is id sheasamh,
Airde mo ghlún, is chomh luath so ag 'meacht uaim!

Is fada an ród é le triall agat feasta,
Is ceangal na mbróg ort níl ann ach tús ceangail.

The First Shoes

for John David

We put his shoes on for the first time this morning,
Neat and snug, the best of leather,
A miracle of shoemaking to adorn
The little feet that ran free till now,
The first shoes ever on the little honey steps.

Bend these fine shoes to your will,
My little treasure, strike the ground firmly,
Lift your darling head bravely, boldly,
Little man who can stand and walk tall,
The height of my knee and already leaving me!

You have a long road to travel yet,
And the spancel of shoes is only the first.

(PS)

Gráinne

Do chuireadar fios ar inín an rí
Óna súgradh caoin ar chiumhais na habhann
Teacht fé dhéin a hathar gan mhoill
Go snaidhmfí cuing léi idir dhá namhaid.

Do sheasaimh an rí i ngeata na Teamhrach,
A mheabhair á suathadh ag cúrsaí cleamhnais,
Ag feitheamh le filleadh don rín is dá complacht
Mar scata fáinleog i dtús an tsamhraidh.

Ba chlos a glórsan thar gach glór dó
Is ba léir dó i bhfad uaidh a siúl dob éadrom;
Ní raibh sí stuama múinte mómhar,
Ach gáireach mar ba dhual dá haos bheith…

Ach mar bheadh ré i measc na réilteann,
Nó ar ghrean na trá mar bheadh péarla,
Nó mar rós úr ar lomaghéaga,
Do bhí sí siúd i measc a gaolbhan.

Níor bhog a chroí ar theacht ina ghaor di
Le trua dá hóige ná dá háilleacht;
Fé dhual dá gruaig chas barra méire
Is dúirt, 'Tá do chleamhnas déanta, a Ghráinne.'

Cárbh fhios di siúd cad é bhí roimpi
Nuair d'umhlaigh sí dá thoil go dílis?
Mearbhall grá agus seachrán oíche
Agus éad ban Éireann go lá na scríbe.

Gráinne

They called the king's daughter
From where she played by the river.
She was needed, as a tie, to bind
Adversaries together.

The king stood waiting at Tara's gate
Working out the implications
Of the match he had made, till the princess came
In a flight of swallow maidens.

He heard her voice above the rest
From afar, recognised her carriage.
She wasn't obedient, quiet, tame.
She laughed as one of her age laughs.

But she was moon among the stars,
Pearl in shifting sea sands,
Single rose on a naked branch,
As she came with all her companions.

His heart was hard and didn't move
With pity for youth or beauty.
He twisted his finger into her hair:
'Your match is made, Gráinne.'

As she bowed to his will, did she realise
What would follow after:
Blinding love, ceaseless wandering,
The eternal envy of the women of Ireland?

(BJ)

An seanghalar

Cad a bhí it éadan go ngéillfinnse dod bhréithre?
Níor dheineas ort ach féachaint is do thréig mo chiall;
Claondearc na súl nglas, do choiscéim ab éadrom,
Do chéasadar mo chroíse, is go réidh ní chuirfead díom.

    Is, a chaológánaigh, ba chráite an mhaise dhuit
    Teacht aniar aduaidh orm go cúthail i ngan fhios dom —
    Caidreamh go dtí seo riamh níor braitheadh eadrainn
    Ach malartú beannacht leat ag gabháil dúinn chun an Aifrinn.

Ógmhná na dúthaí seo, má ritheadar id dhiaidh,
Má thiteadar le baois duit, nár chuma liom a gcás?
Beag dá bharr anois agam suite cois an chlaí
Ag feitheamh féach an bhfeicfinn thú tharam chun na trá.

    Is a chaológánaigh, is fada liom an tseachtain seo,
    Is gach greim bídh dá n-ithimse is láidir ná go dtachtann mé —
    A Dhia mhóir na glóire, ní fiú bheith beo mar mhairimse!
    Is nach crosta é an grá so don té a raghadh gafa ann?

Mar leoithne úr ón bhfarraige i meirfean an lae
Airím do theacht in aice liom, is is gile liom ná bláth
Na bhflaige mbuí san abhainn uaim á leathadh féin le gréin
Aon amharc ort — is nárbh fhearra dhom dá bhfanfá uaim go brách!

    Is a chaológánaigh, do réifeadh dom fáil scartha leat —
    Cleamhnas dom do dhéanfadh mo mhuintir i bhfad as so;
    Salmaireacht na cléire, sácraimint na heaglaise,
    Do thabharfaidís chun céille mé — dá mb'fhéidir liom tú dhearmad.

The Old Complaint

What was in your face made me yield when you spoke?
I only looked upon you and my sense was destroyed;
The grey eyes' crooked glance, the light-footed gait,
They wounded my heart and I'll never again be whole.

And O slender young man, it's a grievous victory
Stealing up to catch me softly before I knew —
Not a word between us was ever noticed till now
Only a greeting if we met on the road to Mass.

If the girls of this townland all ran after you
If they were foolish about you, what was their fate to me?
How does that help me now, sitting beside the fence
Waiting for you to pass me going down to the strand.

And O slender young man this week is long for me
Not a bite I eat but it nearly chokes me —
God in heaven, it's not worth living as I live now!
Love is a misfortune once it takes sure hold.

Like a fresh breeze from the sea in the hot part of the day
I feel you coming near me, and brighter than the flower
Of those yellow water irises spreading before the sun
One glimpse of you — and better for me if you stayed away for good!

And O slender young man, I'd be all right if we parted —
My people would arrange a match somewhere far away;
The chanting of the clergy, the church's great sacrament
Would bring me to my wits again — if I could forget your face.

(EC)

Suantraí Ghráinne

Codail, a laoich dar thugas grá,
Codail go sámh im bhánbhaclainn,
Tusa mo rogha thar thogha fear Fáil.
Thar rí na bhFian is a chóir fairis —
    Codail, codail, a chúl na lúb,
    Le faobhar na hoíche, codail, a rún.

Is mó rí tíre agus ceannaire cúige
A luífeadh le fonn anocht id leaba;
Dhe rogha, ná sínfeá féin, a rún,
Gan céile id chlúid i measc an aitinn —
    Ach codail, óir fós ní baol duit san,
    Codail gan ceo, a mhuirnín ban.

Seachain, a sheanabhroic liaith ón gcnoc,
Seachain, a shionnaigh chríonna an fhill,
Fágaig'se fúinne an áit seo anocht,
A shluaite a mhaireann fé scairt i gcoill —
    Is codail go fóill, a chroí im chléibh,
    Go héirí gréine de dhroim sléibhe.

Codail, a laoich dar thugas grá,
Codail go sámh is do cheann lem ucht,
Mise a thug ort dianseachrán,
Mise a fhairfidh do shuan anocht —
    Codail, codail, a mhian gach mná,
    Codail, a mhaoin, roimh theacht don lá.

Gráinne's Lullaby

Sleep, hero that I have loved.
Sleep untroubled in the crook of my white arm.
You were my choice from the choicest of Ireland's men —
Over the king of the Fianna and his corps.
      Sleep, sleep my curly-haired.
      At the edge of night, sleep my dear one.

Many's the king of a country, many's the province's headman
Would gladly sleep in your bed tonight.
You'd as soon lay your limbs, my dear,
Uncompanioned, in your shelter among the gorse,
      But sleep, for that's no risk to you yet.
      Sleep without trouble, darling of women.

Beware, old grey badger of the hill.
Beware, treacherous old fox.
And you many who live in woods under thickets,
Leave this place to us tonight.
      Sleep a while yet — you, my heart within,
      Till the sun shows over the mountain ridge.

Sleep, hero that I have loved.
Sleep easy, your head on my breast.
I who have put you to this harsh straying —
It is I who'll watch over your sleeping this night.
      Sleep. Desire of every woman, sleep.
      Sleep my treasure till day comes.

(AH)

A fhir dar fhulaingeas…

A fhir dar fhulaingeas grá fé rún,
Feasta fógraím an clabhsúr:
Dóthanach den damhsa táim,
Leor mo bhabhta mar bhantráill.

Tuig gur toil liom éirí as,
Comhraím eadrainn an costas:
'Fhaid atáim gan codladh oíche
Daorphráinn orchra mh'osnaíle.

Goin mo chroí, gad mo gháire,
Cuimhnigh, a mhic mhínáire,
An phian, an phláigh, a chráigh mé,
Mo dhíol gan ádh gan áille.

Conas a d'agróinnse ort
Claochló gréine ach t'amharc,
Duí gach lae fé scailp dhaoirse —
Malairt bhaoth an bhréagshaoirse!

Cruaidh an cás mo bheith let ais,
Measa arís bheith it éagmais;
Margadh bocht ó thaobh ar bith
Mo chaidreamh ortsa, a óigfhir.

Man for Whom I Endured...

Man, for whom I suffered love
In secret, I now call a halt.
I'll no longer dance in step.
Far too long I've been enthralled.

Know that I desire surcease,
Reckon up what love has cost
In racking sighs, in blighted nights
When every hope of sleep is lost.

Harrowed heart, strangled laughter;
Though you're dead to shame, I charge you
With my luckless graceless plight
And pain that plagues me sorely.

Yet, can I blame you that the sun
Darkens when you are in sight?
Until I'm free each day is dark —
False freedom to swap day for night!

Cruel my fate, if by your side.
Crueller still, if set apart.
A bad bargain either way
To love you or to love you not.

(BJ)

Fógra

’Ógánaigh sin an cheana, dá dtuigtheá tú féin i gceart
Bhraithfeá an bhliain ag caitheamh is na laethanta ag imeacht;
Leat, an fhaid a mhairfidh, an luisne sin i gcneas,
An bláth san ar an leacain, an tathaint sin na ndearc,
Ach ní mór don taoide casadh, is ’sé dán na hoíche teacht.

Chím chughat an tuar ins an uair ná haithneofar
Breáthacht do chlúimhse thar ghearrcaigh na gcomharsan,
Mustar do chúrsa i gcuibhreann ban óg duit,
Crot an chinn chúmtha, ná guaille atá córach
Crochta go huaibhreach fén seanachasóig sin.

Fair tú féin is seachain, ós tú an tarna mac,
Sara dtagthá turas abhaile is ná beadh romhat cead isteach,
Is áilleachtaí do phearsan ná fóirfeadh ort, nár chleacht
Suáilce fós ná carthain is réim an tsrutha leat—
Nuair a theipeann ar an dtaitneamh is tarcaisneach a bhlas.

Cluas dom, a dhalta, is meabhraigh an méid seo,
Is má luír do shúil ar chailín i leith chughat ina dhéidh seo
Ná dein iontas de ná tagann: ba leor uait uair an sméideadh
Ach anois tá dulta amach ort, is do tugadh ort do thréithe,
Is mo thrua í mar a mealladh, más miste thú le héinne.

Warned Off

Young heart-throb, if you knew your own self to rights
You'd feel the years are sliding on, the days passing by;
You'll keep that glow on your skin for as long as it stays bright,
The flower of your complexion, the urgent glance,
But the tide has to turn, and at last comes the night.

I see signs of the time when the flash of your feathers
Will seem no smarter than the country hatchlings,
Paraded in the company of young women,
The fine form of the head, the level shoulders
Arrogantly posed under that ancient coat.

Take care, for you are the second son, and keep in mind,
You might come home one day and not be allowed inside,
Your handsome frame will be no help, you've never learned
Virtue or charity as you floated with the stream —
The day that pleasure fails its taste is despised.

So listen to me, young fellow, and remember what I say,
And from this out if you give a girl your eye
Don't be surprised if she stays put: a wink was once enough
But now your ways are known, your measure is taken,
And I pity the woman deceived, if there's even one who cares for you.

(EC)

An buachaill aimsire

Maidin Dhomhnach Cásca trí ráithe in aontíos sinn —
Is dá mb'é an chéad lá a thánag é, is láidir má bheannaís dom!
Tusa iníon na máistrí 's is mise an seirbhíseach —
        Bíodh agat.

Cén difir ach an t-achar san go rabhas-sa ar fán tíre
Go bhfacasa na máistrí ba mháistrí dáiríre
Is na mná nár chuir ar talamh riamh aon chos gan stoca síoda —
        Is nára maith!

Is ait liom féin an mháithrín nár mhúin duit caint shibhialta
Is is diail an gearradh brád é mar ligeadh cead do chinn leat!
Ná tagadh sé it aigne go mbeinnse ag brú comaoine ort —
        Ná m'aire air.

Mo ghraidhn seacht n-uaire a mhargadh a phósfaidh chun an tí seo!
Níor spalpadh fós an strapaire a bhainfeadh ceart ná riail díot —
Foghlaimeoidh sé peannaid uait nach cúiteamh acaraí ann —
        Ní mise san.

Fágfadsa an baile seo de réir mar a rúnaíonn dom,
An ainnise is an salachar agus síorchur na báistí ann;
Ní péacóg bheag ar bhuaile a choimeádfaidh i bhfonsaí mé —
        Creid mé leat.

Atá mo riar i Sasana is is f'riste teacht i dtír ann,
Tuillfead mo chuid airgid is socaireoidh mé síos ann
Gan stró orm ná aithreachas — ach anso a bheirse choíche
        Led chliamhain isteach.

The Servant Boy

Easter Sunday morning, we're in the one house three seasons —
And as if it were my first day here you barely give me greeting!
You're the master's daughter, who cares how the hired man's treated —
      Have your own way.

What odds barring the miles from when I wandered abroad
Where I could see masters then that were genuine lords,
Ladies that never put a foot without silk stocking on the ground —
      Unlike you!

I wonder your mamma didn't teach you to speak civil,
But they gave you your own way and you're going to the devil!
Never think I have in mind to be looking for your favour —
      Perish the thought.

The man that marries into this house will get a desperate bargain!
The hero hasn't yet appeared that could keep you in order
You'll make him suffer more than those fields are worth —
      It won't be me.

I've settled in my own mind to leave this place behind me,
The mess and the misfortune and the rain that would blind you;
No little peacock in her little pen will cramp my style now —
      Believe you me.

My plans are made for England, getting on there is easy,
I'll earn my share of money and I'll settle where I please there:
No bother, no regrets — but you'll stay forever here, with
      Your match, married in.

(EC)

Cad is bean?

Gránna an rud í an bhean,
      hOileadh casta,
Díreach seach claon ní fheadair,
      Bréag a n-abair;

Níl inti ceart ná náire,
      Níl inti glaine,
An ghin ón gcléibh tá meata,
      Mar is baineann;

Beatha dhi inneach an duine,
      Slán ní scarfair
Go gcoillfidh agat gach tearmann,
      Go bhfágfaidh dealbh;

Cleachtadh an tsúmaire a sampla,
      Go maireann amhlaidh,
'Mise glacsam!' a paidir,
      Ampla a foghlaim:

Mar tá sí gan céim chumais
      Ach i mbun millte,
Nimh léi gach fiúntas dearbh
      Phréamhaigh sa tsaoirse;

Chás di cumann a chúiteamh,
      Ní heol di féile,
Má d'imir ina reic a pearsain
      Is le fíoch éilimh;

What Is Woman?

Reprehensible is woman,
       Reared awry. She
Proper from improper knows not,
       Tells lies.

Nor truth, nor shame
       In her, nor cleanliness;
From conception, weak
       In her womanness.

No escape from her. She
       Battens on guts and garters,
Violates every sanctuary,
       Leaves only bare carcass.

The leech taught her a trade
       And she lives by it,
'Give, give' is her prayer
       Greed her learning.

Accomplished at nothing
       But sheer destruction
She despises all virtue
       Rooted in freedom.

Reluctant to return favour
       She gives, grudgingly.
If she gambles her body
       She expects a high return.

Tá gann, tá cúng, tá suarach,
    Gan sásamh i ndán di
Ach an déirc is an tsíoraithis —
    Dar marthain! is gránna.

Mean, tight and narrow. She
    Is never easy, relentlessly
Demanding, abusive,
    And utterly reprehensible.

(BJ)

Ceathrúintí Mháire Ní Ógáin

I

Ach a mbead gafa as an líon so —
Is nár lige Dia gur fada san —
B'fhéidir go bhfónfaidh cuimhneamh
Ar a bhfuaireas de shuaimhneas id bhaclainn

Nuair a bheidh ar mo chumas guíochtaint,
Comaoine is éisteacht Aifrinn,
Cé déarfaidh ansan nach cuí dhom
Ar 'shonsa is ar mo shon féin achaine?

Ach comhairle idir dhá linn duit,
Ná téir ródhílis in achrann,
Mar go bhfuilimse meáite ar scaoileadh
Pé cuibhrinn a snaidhmfear eadrainn.

II

Beagbheann ar amhras daoine,
Beagbheann ar chros na sagart,
Ar gach ní ach bheith sínte
Idir tú agus falla —

Neamhshuim liom fuacht na hoíche,
Neamhshuim liom scríb is fearthainn,
Sa domhan cúng rúin teolaí seo
Ná téann thar fhaobhar na leapan —

Ar a bhfuil romhainn ní smaoinfeam,
Ar a bhfuil déanta cheana,
Linne an uain, a chroí istigh,
Is mairfidh sí go maidin.

Mary Hogan's Quatrains

I

O to be disentangled from this net —
And may God not let that be long —
Perhaps the memory will help
Of all the ease I had in your arms.

When I shall have the ability to pray,
Take communion and hear Mass,
Who will say then that it is not seemly
To intercede on yours and on my own behalf?

But meanwhile my advice to you,
Don't get too firmly enmeshed,
For I am determined to let loose
Whatever bond between us is tied.

II

I care little for people's suspicions,
I care little for priests' prohibitions,
For anything save to lie stretched
Between you and the wall —

I am indifferent to the night's cold,
I am indifferent to the squall or rain,
When in this warm narrow secret world
Which does not go beyond the edge of the bed —

We shall not contemplate what lies before us,
What has already been done,
Time is on our side, my dearest,
And it will last till morning.

III

Achar bliana atáim
Ag luí farat id chlúid,
Deacair anois a rá
Cad leis a raibh mo shúil!

Ghabhais de chosaibh i gcion
A tugadh go fial ar dtúis,
Gan aithint féin féd throigh
Fulaing na feola a bhrúigh!

Is fós tá an creat umhal
Ar mhaithe le seanagheallúint,
Ach ó thost cantain an chroí
Tránn áthas an phléisiúir.

IV

Tá naí an éada ag deol mo chíchse,
Is mé ag tál air de ló is d'oíche;
An garlach gránna ag cur na bhfiacal,
Is de nimh a ghreama mo chuisle líonta.

A ghrá, ná maireadh an trú beag eadrainn,
Is a fholláine, shláine a bhí ár n-aithne;
Barántas cnis a chloígh lem chneas airsin,
Is séala láimhe a raibh gach cead aici.

Féach nach meáite mé ar chion a shéanadh,
Cé gur sháigh an t-amhras go doimhin a phréa'cha;
Ar láir dhea-tharraic ná déan éigean,
Is díolfaidh sí an comhar leat ina séasúr féinig.

V

Is éachtach an rud í an phian,
Mar chaitheann an cliabh,

III

For the space of a year I have been
Lying with you in your embrace,
Hard to say now
What I was hoping for!

You trampled on love,
That was freely given at first,
Unaware of the suffering
Of the flesh you crushed under foot.

And yet the flesh is willing
For the sake of an old familiar pledge,
But since the heart's singing has ceased
The joy of pleasure ebbs.

IV

The child of jealousy is sucking my breast,
While I nurse it day and night;
The ugly brat is cutting teeth,
My veins throb with the venom of its bite.

My love, may the little wretch not remain between us,
Seeing how healthy and full was our knowledge of each other;
It was a skin warranty that kept us together,
And a seal of hand that knew no bounds.

See how I am not determined to deny love,
Though doubt has plunged its roots deep;
Do not force a willing mare,
And she will recompense you in her own season.

V

Pain is a powerful thing,
How it consumes the breast,

Is ná tugann faoiseamh ná spás
Ná sánas de ló ná d'oích' —

An té atá i bpéin mar táim
Ní raibh uaigneach ná ina aonar riamh,
Ach ag iompar cuileachtan de shíor
Mar bhean gin féna coim.

VI

'Ní chodlaím istoíche' —
Beag an rá, ach an bhfionnfar choíche
Ar shúile oscailte
Ualach na hoíche?

VII

Fada liom anocht!
Do bhí ann oíche
Nárbh fhada faratsa —
Dá leomhfainn cuimhneamh.

Go deimhin níor dheacair san,
An ród a d'fhillfinn —
Dá mba cheadaithe
Tréis aithrí ann.

Luí chun suilt
Is éirí chun aoibhnis
Siúd ba chleachtadh dhúinn —
Dá bhfaighinn dul siar air.

It gives no respite day or night,
It gives no peace or rest —

Anyone who feels pain like me,
Has never been lonely or alone,
But is ever bearing company
Like a pregnant woman, in her womb.

VI

'I do not sleep at night' —
Of no account, but will we ever know
With open eyes
The burden of the night?

VII

Tonight seems never-ending!
There was once such a night
Which with you was not long —
Dare I call to mind.

That would not be hard, for sure,
The road on which I would return —
If it were permitted
After repentance.

Lying down for joy
And rising to pleasure
That is what we practised —
If only I could return to it.

(JG)

An dá thráigh

Tuileann an léan im choim
Mar theilgeann fuarán fé chloich;
Mé ag iompar na croise dúinn dís
Ó scaras led bhéal anocht.
Is mé an leanbh baineadh den gcín,
Is mé an lao — is an té do scoith.

An chuisle mhear ag gabháil tríom
Ní réidh dom staonadh óna sruth
Is do phéinse is stalcadh íota
Ná féadaim tál air le deoch.
Is mé tobar searbh ar shliabh,
Is mé foinse an uisce is goirt.

Gach ar agraíos riamh
Mar chomharthaí dearfa ar chion,
Ní hionann sa scála iad
Led chur ó dhoras mar seo —
Is mé an mháthair sháraigh a broinn;
Níor leoite marthain don rud!

The Two Ebbs

Anguish courses through me
As a fountain gushes from below ground;
I carry the cross for both of us
Since I parted from your lips tonight.
I am the child torn from the breast.
I am the calf — and the one who tore it away.

Not easy for me to abstain
From the current pulsing through me
And your pain a parching thirst
On which I couldn't bestow a dram.
I am a bitter well on a mountain.
I am the source of brackish water.

All that I ever swore
As true signs of affection,
In no way compares
To banishing you like this —
I am the mother who thwarted her womb;
The thing didn't stand a chance.

(CF)

Cian á thógaint díom

Do mheabhair is mó anois a bhraithim uaim —
Ní cuí dhom feasta cumann rúin an tsúsa —
Cleamhnas na hintinne, ná téann i ndísc,
A d'fhág an t-éasc im lár, an créacht ná dúnann.

An mó de bhlianaibh scartha dhúinn go beacht
Roimh lasadh im cheann don láchtaint seo taibhríodh dom?
Téann díom, ach staonfad fós den gcomhaireamh seasc,
Altaím an uain is ní cheistím an faoiseamh.

Milse ár gcomhluadair d'fhill orm trém néall,
Cling do chuileachtan leanann tréis na físe,
Do leath ár sonas tharainn mar an t-aer,
Bheith beo in éineacht, fiú gan cnaipe 'scaoileadh.

Do cheannfhionn dílis seirgthe i gcré
An t-éitheach; is an fíor? An aisling ghlé.

Sorrow Lifts from Me

More than anything, it's your mind I feel the loss of now.
The love between the sheets has had its day
But the bond of mind, which never fades
Is what tears me, is the wound that never heals.

How many years exactly since we parted
Before this brightening kindled like a waking dream?
I can't remember, and will not count them, but
Give thanks for the moment and not question its peace.

The sweetness of our company came back to me in the dream,
The chime of your pleasure still sounds in the room,
Our joy spread round us like the air.
Even if no button is undone, just to be alive together.

This is the lie: your fair head withered in clay.
And the truth? The clear vision in the brightening day.

(PS)

An bhean mhídhílis

ó Spáinnis García Lorca

Is gur thugas liom í 'on abhainn
Á cheapadh ná raibh ach ina cailín
Nuair a bhí aici céile.

Oíche San Seoin a bhí ann
Agus fé mar tharlódh sé le coinne
Do múchadh soilse na sráide
Is do thóg na cnaitheacha tine.
Ag tiontú na gcúinní deireanach
Leagas mo lámh ar a cíocha
Is do mhúscail chugham óna gcodladh
Mar osclann bláth na n-iasainteach.
Ba chlos dom an treisín ina cóta
Mar a bheadh leithead síoda
Á scríobadh le deich bhfaobhair scine
Ag gabháil lem ais ins an tslí dhi.
Gan airgead réalach i gcorn,
Tá fásta na crainn 'ár dtimpeall,
Is gadhair i bhfad ón abhainn
In imeall na spéire ag sceamhaíl orainn.
Fágtha 'ár ndiaidh na sceacha
Tá, an duilliúr is an flaige;
Fé ualach a triopall gruaige
Do shocraíos nead ins an ghainimh.
Do scaoileas an carabhat snaidhmthe,
Do lig sí a gúna díthi,
Do scaoileas an crios is an gunna,
Is an chabhail cheathairfhillte.
Lítis, máthair an phéarla,
Níl acu cneas chomh caoin sin,

The Unfaithful Woman

From the Spanish of García Lorca

And so I brought her to the river
Thinking she was but a maiden
When she already had a husband.

It was St John's Eve
And, as though by signal,
The streetlights were quenched
And the fireflies blazed.
Turning the final corners
My hand rested on her breast
And it awoke to me
As a hyacinth opens.
The starch in her coat
Sounded like a length of silk
Rent by ten knife-blades
As she moved alongside me.
With no moonsilver in their cups,
The trees around us had grown
And at the horizon, far from the river,
Hounds were baying at us.
We had left the whitethorn behind,
The foliage and flaggerts;
Under the weight of her mane
I fashioned a nest in the sand.
I loosened the knot in my tie,
She slipped off her dress,
I loosened my belt and gun,
And her four-folded bodice.
Lily white, mother of pearl,
Neither have such soft skin

Ná níl, dá ghile fuinneog ann,
Gléas i ngloine mar bhí sí.
Do leath a ceathrúin fém mhéara
Mar dhá bhreac éisc ag ráthaíocht,
Sciar acu líonta den lasair
Is sciar den bhfuacht is iad líonta.
Creid gur ghabhas-sa an oíche úd
Rogha gach conrach go dtí seo
I muin an tsearraigh ghléghil,
Marcach gan srian gan iarann.
Gach a ndúirt liom os íseal
Ní háil liom, ós fear mé, d'insint.
Solas na tuisceana im intinn
Do mhúin dom measarthacht briathar.
Smeartha lem póga do bhí
Nuair thugas ón abhainn í abhaile.
Do nocht claimhte na ngiolcach
I gcomhrac le leoithne na maidne.

D'iompraíos mé féin mar is cóir
Do stócach ón dtreibh ar díobh mé.
Cheannaíos di bosca fuála
Breá, agus líneáil bhuí ann,
Is níor mhian liom titim i ngrá léi
Ón uair go raibh céile ann di,
Is go ndúirt ná raibh ach ina cailín
Nuair thugas liom chun na habhann í.

Nor, no matter how bright a window,
No glass is as polished as she.
Her thighs parted beneath my fingers,
Like two basking trout
Half filled with flame,
Half filled with frost.
Believe me, I raced that night
On the very best of roads
Astride that sweet filly,
Horseman without rein or stirrup.
All that she whispered to me
I, being a man, will not repeat.
The light of understanding
Taught me the measure of words.
Covered in my kisses
I brought her home from the river.
The tips of the reeds could be seen
Battling the morning breeze.

I behaved as befits
An unwed youth of my tribe.
I bought her a fine sewing box
With yellow lining,
And had no wish to fall in love with her
Since she had a husband,
And said she was but a maiden
When I brought her to the river.

(CF)

Cam reilige 1916–1966

Iadsan a cheap an riail,
'Mheabhraigh an dualgas,
A d'fhág fuarbhlas orainn,
Oidhrí na huachta,
Fé ndear gur leamh anois
Gach ní nach tinneall
Íogair ar fhaobhar lice
Idir dhá thine.

Fear lár an tsúsa
Conas a thuigfeadh san
Oibriú an fhuachta
Ar bhráithre na n-imeallach?
Cár ghaibh ár mbagairt ar
Fhear lár na fichille?
Amas a crapadh ar
Chiosaíbh an imeartha!

Lonnú is fearann dúinn
Bord na sibhialtachta;
Cad a bheir beatha ann
Seachas ar phrínseabal?
Ná caitear asachán
Linne — lucht céalacain —
B'shin a raibh d'acht againn;
Ár gcoir? Gur ghéill ann!

Birth Defect 1916–1966

Those who established the rule,
Reminded us of our duty,
Left us cold, inheritors
Of their legacy, bored
With everything that is not
A precarious trembling
On a knife edge
Between blazing fires.

How can the moderate man
In his comfortable bed
Understand how the cold
Afflicts his brothers on the edge?
What happened all our threats
Against the chessboard king?
Our assault collapsed
On the outskirts of the battlefield!

We have settled down
On the level plain of civilization:
Life here derives from
What else if not principle?
Spare us your contempt.
Deprived of nourishment,
It was our only code.
Our crime? That we accepted it.

(LP)

An fuath (1967)

Is é a dh'éilíonn an fuath fadfhulang
        agus fadaradhna,
Is é a dh'éilíonn an fuath neamhaithne
        agus daille na foighne,
Is é a dh'éilíonn an fuath méar shocair
        ar ghaiste an raidhfil —
Is ná scaoil go bhfeicfir gealadh na súl
        mar ghealacán uibh id radharc uait!

San am a mbláthóidh an fuath troidfear ar
        thrínsí sráide
Is leathfar an ghloine bhriste roimh eacha
        póilíní ar cos in airde —
Ach idir an dá linn, an fuath, is maith an
        leasú é ar ghairdín
Ar dhu'í gain'í idir dhá thaoide —
        mar a maireann ár mná 's ár bpáistí!

Hatred (1967)

Hatred demands patience and deadened senses,
Hatred waits for its chance;
Hatred keeps a steady finger on the trigger
And won't pull it till it sees the whites of the eyes
Like egg-whites in its sights!

When hatred blossoms there will be fighting in the streets
And broken bottles flung at the rearing horses of the riot police;
But in the meantime hatred improves the garden
Built on sand-dunes between two tides —
Where our women and children live.

(PS)

Fód an imris: Ard-Oifig an Phoist, 1986

Anso, an ea, 'athair, a thosnaigh sé?
Gur dhein strainséirí dínn dá chéile?
Anso, an ea?

Fastaím a shílis riamh dár mórchuid cainte—
Fiú nuair aontaíomar leat:

Oidhrí ar eachtra nár aithin bolaith an phúdair
Ná na heagla,
Nár chaith riamh ruchar feirge
Is is lú ná san
A sheas ...

D'éalaíomar uait thar Pháil na Gaelainne isteach;
B'shin *terre guerre* ba linn fhéin,
Is chuaigh sé de mhianach an Olltaigh
Ionatsa
Ár lorg a rianadh,
Ár dtabhairt chun tíríochais—
Civilitie Spenser
D'oibrigh ortsa a chluain.

Leanamarna treabhchas na máthar:
Kranz barrghaoitheach na Mumhan;
Ba tusa an seanabhroc stóinsithe,
Sceamhaíl ort ag paca spáinnéar.

Le haois ghnáthaíomar a chéile thar n-ais;
D'fhoghlaimís carthain,
Ach b'éigean fós siúl go haireach;
Do mheabhair agus th'acfainn chirt

Trouble Spot: General Post Office 1986

Here, father, is this where it started?
Here we became strangers to each other?
Was it here?

You thought most of what we said was nonsense—
Even when we agreed with you:

Inheritors of the event who never knew the smell
Of gunpowder, or of terror,
Who never fired a shot in anger,
Worse yet,
Never stood up to one...

We retreated from you into the Pale of Irish;
That was our familiar *terre guerre*,
And the Ulsterman
In you
Could not follow our tracks
Or tame our barbarism—
Spenser's *civilitie*
Had beguiled you.

We took after our mother's tribe:
The high-blown ways of Munster;
You were the recalcitrant old badger
Run to ground by howling spaniels.

In later years, we tried again;
You learned to be charitable,
But we still had to tread carefully;
Your intelligence and sense of justice

Níor thaithigh cúl scéithe;
Comhaos mé féin is an stát,
Is níor chun do thola do cheachtar.

Óigfhear in easnamh, anaithnid, thú, 'athair,
San áit seo—
Ceileann neamart is tuathal an eochair ar m'intinn—
Ach an seanóir a charas le grá duaisiúil,
Cloisim a thuin aduaidh:
An cuimhin leat an t-aitheasc a thugais
Nuair ná raibh faiseanta fós?
Mar seo do ráidhis é:

I see no cause for rejoicing
That Irishmen once again
Are killing other Irishmen
On the streets of Belfast!

Never practised deception;
I am the same age as the state
And neither turned out as you wished…

In this place, father, you are the unknown
Youth who went missing —
Neglect and awkwardness hide the key from my mind —
But I hear now the Northern accent
Of the elder man I loved with hard devotion:
Do you remember the rebuke you delivered
Before it became fashionable?
You spoke thus:

I see no cause for rejoicing
That Irishmen once again
Are killing other Irishmen
On the streets of Belfast!

(LP)

Iníon a' Lóndraigh

Is go bhfuil comhartha cille ar inín a' Londraigh
Os cionn sál a bróige thiar! — PIARAS FEIRTÉAR

Córach iníon a' Lóndraigh — is ins na blianta d'imigh,
Sarar leath an liath san ómra, sara dtáinig roic 'na leicinn,
Is cuimhin liom nuair ba chóraí …

Leathan as ucht, as chromán, as ghuailne —
Caol a com, a malaí 's a méara —
A cúl dob uaibhreach,
A siúl 's a hiompar
Mar a bheadh bád ag teacht fé éadach,
Ag gabháil na gaoithe
Is taoide léithi.

Ceathrar mac ag an Lóndrach 's an cúigiú duine baineann;
Is an bhean dea-chroí do seoladh
Níor mhair sí le go bhfeicfeadh —
Leasmháthair 'sea do thóg í;
Ní bhfuair taithí na leisce!

Leanann gach ráithe in' uainíocht fhéinig,
Na trátha ag baint ionú dá chéile,
Gur éirigh sí 'na maighdin déanta —
Má dhein, níor thánathas dá héileamh;
Do chuaigh amach ná raibh aon spré léi.

Scéal ar iníon a' Lóndraigh, an planda d'fhás sa bhfothain
Gur iompaigh críon is feoite gan lámh a theacht 'na gaire,
Cé hé anois a neosfaidh?
Ní mise é ná ise —

Landers' Daughter

And Landers' daughter has a little mole
Just there above the heel of her shoe! — PIERCE FERRITER

Landers' daughter still looks well — and in years gone by
Before the grey spread through the amber, before wrinkles
Appeared in her cheeks, I remember she looked better still...

Broad of chest, of hips, and shoulders —
Slender her waist, her eyebrows and fingers —
Her head proud,
Her walk and her carriage
Like a boat under sail
Tacking into the wind
And the tide running with her.

Landers had four sons
And the fifth child was a girl;
The good woman who gave her birth
Never lived to see her —
Reared by a stepmother,
Hers was never the lazy way!

Each season follows in its own time,
Replacing in turn the one before,
Until she was ready to marry —
But no one came to seek her hand;
Word went out that she had no dowry.

This is the story of Landers' daughter, the flower
That grew in a shaded place until it aged and withered
Untouched by any hand.
Who now will tell the tale?
Not I; not she —

Chím uaim insa tsáipéal í
Is ní fios an bhfeadar aoinne
Go rabhamar buíoch dá chéile.

I see her ahead of me in church
And wonder does anyone know
That she and I were great with each other once.

(LP)

Codladh an ghaiscígh

Ceannín mogallach milis mar sméar —
A mhaicín iasachta, a chuid den tsaol,
Dé do bheathasa is neadaigh im chroí
Dé do bheathasa fé fhrathacha an tí,
A réilthín maidine tháinig i gcéin.

Is maith folaíocht isteach!
Féach mo bhullán beag d'fhear;
Sáraigh sa doras é nó ceap
I dtubán — chomh folláin le breac
Gabhaimse orm! Is gach ball fé rath,
An áilleacht mar bharr ar an neart —

Do thugais ón bhfómhar do dhath
Is ón rós crón. Is deas
Gach buí óna chóngas leat.
Féach, a Chonchúir, ár mac,
Ní mar beartaíodh ach mar cheap
Na cumhachta in airde é 'theacht.

Tair go dtím bachlainn, a chircín eornan,
Tá an lampa ar lasadh is an oíche ag tórmach,
Tá an mada rua ag siúl an bóthar,
Nár sheola aon chat mara ag snapadh é id threosa,
Nuair gur tú coinneal an teaghlaigh ar choinnleoirín óir duit.

Id shuan duit fém borlach
Is fál umat mo ghean —
Ar do chamachuaird má sea
Fuar agam bheith dhed bhrath.

Hero Sleeps

Blackberry sweet your little clustered head,
My little stranger son, my share of life,
Welcome here, and settle in my heart.
Welcome under the rafters of this house,
Morning star, come from afar.

What a boon is new blood!
See my small thulking bullman,
Head him off in the doorway,
Or wedge him in a tub — tight as a trout,
I declare! Each limb perfection,
Its beauty a gloss on strength —

Your colouring you took from Autumn,
And from the dark rose. You light
All yellows at your approach.
Look, Conor, our son
Not made to our design but planned
By destinies above.

Come here till I hold you, my barley-chick darling.
Lamps are lighting as night draws in.
The red fox is prowling the road.
May no cat from the sea
Send him snapping towards you,
Who are the lighted candle of this house,
Enthroned on your sconce of gold.

As you sleep beneath my breast
My love is a wall around you —
Out there in the world
You are beyond my care.

Cén chosaint a bhéarfair leat?
Artha? Leabharúin? Nó geas?
'Ná taobhaigh choíche an geal,'
Paidir do chine le ceart.

Ar nós gach máthar seal
Deinim mo mhachnamh thart
Is le linn an mheabhruithe
Siúd spíonóig mhaide id ghlaic!
Taibhrítear dom go pras
An luan láich os do chneas
I leith is gur chugham a bheadh,
Garsúinín Eamhna, Cú na gCleas!

What will you bring to protect you?
A charm? A talisman? A taboo?
'Never trust the white,'
Is the prayer of your people by right.

As mothers must, I worry all angles,
Lost in thought, and then,
With a wooden spoon in your fist,
Hero moon flashing above you,
I see coming towards me,
The houndboy from Eamhain
Cúchulainn of the Feats.

(BJ)

Do phatalóigín gearrchaile

Amhgar is anaithe,
Laethanta sceoin,
Uamhan ar an raidió
Bheannaigh dár bhflós,
Móra roimh ainnirín,
Gleoite 'na pearsainín,
Dheonaigh sí farainne
Fascain is fód.

Gaethe na maidine
Leath sí mar ór,
Bronntasach, scaipitheach,
Banfhlaith fadó —
Claondearc Éabha an abhallúird
Mheall croí a hathar uaidh,
D'aithin sí Mama, níor
Chéil uirthi cóir.

Créatúirín banúil
Nár éiligh thar meon!
Maith faillí m'aire dhom,
Tuig liom go fóill —
Ná goilleadh Pádraig peata ort,
Déanfam araon an t-aicsean air —
Do mhac do mhac go bpósfaidh,
Ach t'iníon t'iníon go deo!

To a Soft Little Girl

Days of terror,
Distress and dread,
Fear on the radio
Welcomed our flower,
Greetings to the maiden,
Charming little mite,
Who bestowed on us also
Shelter and sod.

The rays of the morning
She spread as though gold,
Magnanimous, bountiful,
A princess of old —
With the lazy eye of apple-famed Eve,
She beguiled her Dad,
Mindful of Mama, never shrank
From granting her her due.

A little creature of a girl
Who never demanded too much!
Forgive me if I've neglected you,
Bear with me yet —
Don't be put out by Patrick the pet,
Together we'll put him in his place —
Your son your son till he weds
But your daughter your daughter forever!

(CF)

Ceangal do cheol pop

Ait liom go ngeofá slán uaim!
Éaló uaim thar farraige sall!
Is go bhfuilim i gcónaí it ampar
Beagáinín os chionn an ghabhail —
San áit a neadódh an páiste
Dá mbeadh aon pháiste ann!

Outro to a Pop Song

Strange that you should escape me!
Across the sea, unharmed!
While I still carry you
Just here above my crotch —
Where the child might have nested
If there had been a child!

(LP)

Gníomhartha corpartha na trócaire

Chuas ar thuairisc na seanamhná san óspaidéal —
Bhí an t-éadach caite anuas den leabaidh aici,
Bhí a léine oíche éalaithe in airde fána coim,
Truamhéil a bléine liaite, scáinte —
Samhlaíodh sicín ag dul dó 'on oigheann dom —
'A 'níon ó,' ar sise, 'tá an iomarca plaincéadaí anuas orm!'

Bhí an bheirt leanbh crapaithe ar chlár an droichid
Gorm ón bhfuacht —
Gomh in oíche na cathrach —
Thugas mo mhiasam uaim is dúrt,
'Bailíg' libh anois abhaile as so!'
Ní ligfeadh dóibh eagla —
'Fios ar na gardaí,' ars' an fear ag gabháil tharam —
Bhíodar glanta as mo radharc mar thit an sneachta ar an adharta!

Bím i gcónaí ag teitheadh roimpi,
I bpoll tarathair más gá san —
Ba gheall le déirc fanúint léi
D'fhonn babhta comhráidh léi —
Ach ó d'imigh an gluaisteán san thar a maicín mánla
Níl ach an t-aon ábhar cainte amháin aici —
Is bíonn imshníomh orm go gcoireoidh sí mo bheirtse
I mbarr a sláinte.

Bhíodh fáilte isteach roimh chlann na gcomharsan —
Tá sneá anois i gceann Phádraig is caithfear a bhearradh!

The Corporal Works of Mercy

I went to visit the old woman in hospital —
She had thrown the clothes down off the bed,
Her nightdress had slipped up around her waist,
The pathos of her loins was scant and grey —
I thought, a chicken ready for the oven —
'Daughter dear,' she said, 'I have too many blankets on top of me!'

The two children crouched on the crown of the bridge,
Blue with the cold —
The city night was bitter —
I made my contribution and said,
'Off with you home now out of this!'
But fear restrained them —
'Send for the Guards!' said the passer-by —
They were clean out of sight, like snow that fell on the hearth-stone!

I am always running away from her,
Up an auger-hole if need be —
It would be a kindness to wait for her
For some short conversation —
But since that car ran over her gentle little son
She has only the one subject to talk of —
And I fear she will blight my own pair
In their health and strength.

The neighbours' children were always welcome —
Now there are nits in Patrick's hair and it will have to be cut!

(MM)

Cré na mná tí

Coinnibh an teaghlach geal
Agus an chlann fé smacht,
Nigh agus sciúr agus glan,
Cóirigh proinn agus lacht,
Iompaigh tochta, leag brat,
Ach, ar nós Sheicheiriseáide,
Ní mór duit an fhilíocht chomh maith!

The Housewife's Credo

Keep the house tidy,
The family in order,
Wash, scrub, clean,
Get food and drink,
Turn bedding, shake the mat.
And, like Scheherazade,
Add poetry to that.

(BJ)

Love has pitched his mansion…

An cailín mánla deoranta nár dhual di an obair tháir seo,
Do tháinig sí croíleonta le héileamh chugham ón mháthair;
'Comhairigh an uile ghiobal beag a bhaineann le mo pháiste,
Cuntais iad go scrupallach, ná fág aon loc gan áireamh,
Má fhanann oiread 's bríste amú, tá an lios i ngreim im bábán —
Is dá fhaid ó bhaile a scarfam iad, 'sea is mó dá chionn a thnáthfaidh!'

'Ním agus glanaim,' ar seisean, 'agus scagaim mo dhá láimh Ann!'…
I mbríste beag an cheana, banúil, breacaithe le blátha;
Cuirim tríd an sobal é, rinseáilim agus fáiscim —
Níl naomh a thuigfeadh m'aigne 'stighse ach ab é Píoláit é!
Solas na bhflaitheas dá anam bocht go ngnóthaí an níochán so!
        Amen!

Aithis chun scrín na baindé gur tearmann di an t-ard beag!
Do stolladh fiail an teampaill mar do thairngir an fáidh é!
Scaoilim an t-iarann ar an éadach is is clos dom an t-éamh ag Reáime —
Agus tugaim uaim an t-altram is a balcaisí pacáilte…
De gháire na nathrach seanda, de gháire na leasmháthar!

Love has pitched his mansion...

The gentle foreign girl unfit for such rough work
Came to me hurt with demands from the mother:
'Count up every scrap of clothes belonging to my child,
Reckon them scrupulously, leave no rag out of the sum.
If a pair of knickers goes astray, the *lios* will have her always;
Far as we move away the more she'll fail to thrive...'

'*I clean, I wash,*' says he, '*and cleanse my hands of Him!*'
In little lovely knickers, girlish, patterned with flowers:
I put them through the lather, I rinse them and I wring—
No saint would understand what I go through, but Pontius Pilate!
May this washing rest his poor soul!
        Amen!

An insult to the goddess-shrine, whose sanctuary is on a height!
The veil of the temple was torn as the prophet foretold!
I run the iron over the cloth, I hear the wail of Ramah—
I send away the fosterchild, her clothes packed and ready,
And I laugh like the ancient serpent, the laugh of the fostermother.

(EC)

Máiréad sa tsiopa cóirithe gruaige

teideal le caoinchead ó Ghabriel Rosenstock

Chúig mbliana d'aois! Mo phlúirín ómra!
Nár bhaoth an mhaise dhom t'fholt a chóiriú!
Ó do ghaibhis go mánla chun na mná bearrabóra,
Fé dheimheas, fé shobal, fé bhioráin, fé chócaire,
So-ranna, sobhéasach, dea-mhaitheasach, deontach,
Mar uan chun a lomtha is a bhreasaltha i bpóna,
Gur tharraingís talamh id ghearrabhean ghleoite,
Id Shirley Temple, ach a bheith griandóite,
Is gur nocht an scáthán chughat an dealramh nó so…
Golfairt mar chuala nár chloisead go deo arís!
D'fholaís do ghnúis im bolg id sceon duit —
Ábhar do sceimhle ní cheilfead gurb eol dom:
Chughat an fhuil mhíosta, an cumann, an pósadh,
An t-iompar clainne is gaiste an mhóramha…
Mo ghraidhn do chloigeann beag is do ghlóire chorónach
I ngabhal do mháthar ag fúscadh deora
Le fuath don mbaineann is gan fuascailt romhat ann!
A mhaoinín mh'anama, dá bhféadfainn d'fhónfainn.

Margaret in the Hairdressers

Title with thanks to Gabriel Rosenstock

Five years old! My amber flower!
It was foolish of me to fix your hair
So lightly you stepped to the hairdresser
To be soaped and scissored, pinned and dried
With such good grace, willing and obliging
As a lamb to its raddle for shearing and marking
Until you landed on earth like Shirley Temple,
Though not so pale, a charming girl,
Before the mirror revealed the new you ... and then
Oh such lamentation may I never hear again!
With your head in my lap you wept your fill —
I won't pretend I don't know what horrified you:
Love, marriage, the monthly blood, all
Staring back, childbearing, the common lot.
Bless your little head and your crowning glory
As you bawl your eyes out at your mother's waist
With hatred for the female and no escape from it!
My soul's treasure, if only I could help you I would.

(PS)

Fómhar na farraige

Sheo linn ar thórramh an Gharlaigh Choileánaigh
Is i ndoras an tseomra bhí romhainn an mháithrín,
'A mhaicín ó,' ar sí, 'ní raibh críne i ndán duit
Is is dual don óige bheith fiáin ráscánta —
    Is ochón!'…

Fíoghar ar mo shúile iad cneácha míofara a mic,
Is snagaíl fhiata a ghlóir tha is tinn trém chluasaibh —
An gearrcach gránna an dá uair báite againn,
Greas insa tsrúill is greas fén mbladar tomtha —
    Is ochón!

Lasann 'na ghnúis chugham an dá shméaróid dhóite;
Rian na gcúig mhéar mo leiceadarsa tharraing
Tráth gabhadh é is a ladhar aige sa phróca…
Is duitse atáim á insint, a phoill an fhalla!
    Is ochón!

'gCloistí an mháthair? 'Fé mar chaith sé liomsa!
Is tréis gur fhág príosún d'fhill ar an bhfaoistin'…
Do scar an mh'rúch a folt glasuaithne ar Chonaing —
D'fhuadaigh ó fhód na croiche an cincíseach!
    Is ochón!

Amhantarán ón gceallúraigh in' aithbhreith
Ag sianaíl choíche ar rian na daonnachta!
Iarlais ins a' tsíog gaoithe ar neamhmbeith!
Coillteán na trua ón aithis dhéanach so!
    Is ochón!

Harvest of the Sea

We set off to the wake of our whelpish neighbour —
In the bedroom door stood his Mammy waiting —
'O little son,' said she, 'age was not your portion,
And youth is wont to be wild and rakish —
       And ochone!'

My sight retains his scabby features,
His nagging, eerie whine aches through my hearing —
Drown we the scaldy bastard yet again then:
Once in the tide-race, and again in praising —
       And ochone!

I've seen those eyes there, fiery, like embers burning,
Track of five fingers my slap drew across them,
Who caught him with his fist wedged in the crock-mouth —
Hole in the wall, to you I tell my burden!
       And ochone!

Hark to the mother, 'how he treated me, though!
And after he left gaol, went to confession!'
The sea-wife's blue-green hair spread over Conaing —
Wrapt from the gallows-foot the Whitsun weanling!
       And ochone!

Unbaptised, reincarnate by mistake,
Coveting human substance, ever wailing,
In fairy wind annihilated, changeling,
And still insulted, pitiful, castrated —
       And ochone.

Ná bí ag brath ormsa, 'ainniseoir!
Id cháilíocht fhéin dob ann duit dá shuaraí í —
Ach ní réitíonn an marbh is an beo
Hook your own ground! Ní mise bard do chaointe —
      Is ochón!

Éignigh a ghreim den ngunail — bíodh acu!
Cuir suas an t-íomhá céireach i measc na gcoinneal,
An féinics gléasta tar éis a thonachtha,
Is téadh an giobal scéite síos go grinneall —
      Is ochón! ...

Scéal uaim ar thórramh an Gharlaigh Choileánaigh,
Níor facathas fós dúinn aon tsochraid chomh breá léi,
Cliar agus tuath is an dubh ina bhán ann —
Is bearna a' mhíl i bhfolach fén gclár ann —
      Is ochón.

Do not depend on me, wretch, don't come near me —
In your own right, though sordid, you existed —
But dead and living do not suit together —
'Hook your own ground!' I'm not the bard to keen you —
         And ochone!

Force his grip from the gunwale — let them win!
Put up the waxen image — light the candles —
Phoenix arrayed after his death-washing!
And let the spent rag sink to the sea-bottom —
         And ochone!

Tell the tale, how they waked him, the graceless youngster —
Faith, the funeral they gave him was surely a wonder —
Black was made white there, by clergy and laymen,
And the coffin-lid covered, for ever, the hare-lip —
         And ochone!

(MM)

Bás mo mháthar

An dá shúil uaine ar nós na farraige
Cruaidh mar an chloch,
Ag tarrac caol di ar thíos na beatha
      Gan farasbarr,
Ní rabhadar gairdeach, muirneach fá mo choinne:
        Ná rabhas-sa gafa feasta ar shlua na namhad?
Ag díbirt m'athar uaithi! Ag comhairliú réasúin!…

Ní mar sin a samhlaítí dom an bhris,
Ach maoithneach, lán de dhóchas, daite pinc
Le grian tráthnóna, blátha, crónán cliar.
M'aghaidh lena gnúis, mo lámh i ngreim a láimhe,
Shaothróinn di — caiseal tola — cúirt na bhflaitheas,
Is teann an éithigh chrochfadh na geataí
Sa múrtha: ní bheadh teora lem ghaibhneoireacht!
Ní dhruidfeadh léithi oíche an neamhní
Roimh éag don aithne — Ní mar síltear bítear:
Do chros an Dia nach ann Dó an fealladh deiridh!

My Mother's Death

Green as the sea her eyes
And hard as stone
Hoarding what little was left
        Of life's store,
They showed no pleasure or affection when they saw me:
        Had I not joined the ranks of her enemies?
Banishing my father from her! Insisting she be reasonable!...

This is not how I imagined heartbreak;
But rather, sentimental, full of hope, pink
In the evening light; flowers, priestly murmuring.
My face pressed to hers, our hands clasped together,
I would earn — a fortress of desire — heaven's kingdom for her,
And the ultimate deceit would lift the drawbridge
In its walls: there would be no limit to my smithwork!
The night of oblivion would not reach her
Before consciousness died — a fool's paradise:
The God who does not exist prevented the final treachery!

(LP)

You can't win

Aréir do chleachtas-sa im leabaidh aonair
Lánúnas rabharta arís den gcéad uair
Tréis na hóspairte mhartraigh go héag mé...
    Is dom nárbh atuirseach:
Le teann fuarchúise gan spleáchas d'aoinne,
A ndleacht fadchealaithe ba chuimhin lem mhéara
    Ar thóir an taithithe:

Fuaidreán cláirseora ar shreanga teanna,
Cúrsáil bhádóra in ithe an bhealaigh,
Máinneáil éidreorach ó iúl go haithne,
Trí dhiamhair choille, go himeall claise,
'Nar tharraing fá dheoidh an seanabhaile
Gur shrois ceann sprice an aistir fhada
Is i mbaineanntais láibe gur aimsigh cnaipe...

Ó bhonn go baithis tinneall pléisiúra!
A bhlas im béal, a cheol im chluasa!
An dordán meacha! An scaoi! An scuaine!
Tonn ar mhuin toinne a scuab thar buaic mé!
    Is dom nárbh atuirseach!
Gach spreang is scriú im leathchois mhaide
Gur lig gíoscán mar thine chreasa —
Dhiúltaigh don uain le drannadh snagach —
D'aithníos mé féin arís im bheathaidh —
    Faraor, faoi atuirse!

You can't win

Last night, alone in bed, I produced
Flood tides of conjugation for the first time
Since the crippling accident almost killed me…
      And was all the better for it.
In cold blood, no thanks to anyone,
Fingers, seeking what they had known,
        Found their rights, long witheld.

Harper's tentative touch on taut strings.
Boatman, steering through shoals,
Unsteady course from knowing to knowledge
Through dark woods to deep ravine
Drawing slowly towards home.
Final destination,
In female unctions. Button…

Top to toe pleasure's engine.
Taste and hearing engage,
Drone of bees! Swarms and squadrons!
Wave after wave, I surfed
      And was all the better for it!
Every spring and screw in my wooden leg
Struck sparks —
The moment rejected with a jagged snarl —
I found myself alive again —
      And, alas, none the better of it.

(BJ)

Amach san aois

'Le linn m'óige dhom,' ar sise,
'Bhí airgead gann, agus bhí m'aire uile ar scléip na súl;
Ní chuimhneoinn choíche,' ar sise,
'Ar mhus ná ar thúis a cheannach i mbuidéal.
Anois nuair 'amharcann
Bean mhíghnaoithiúil, thonnaosta ón scáthán chugham thar n-ais,
Raidim an chumhracht nódh so ar fuaid mo chliabhraigh
Agus, faoim' shúile iata, airím bolaith an ghrá…
Bolaith an ghrá insa doircheacht,' ar sise,
'Agus bolaith an bháis.'

Old Age

'When I was young,' she said,
'Money was tight, and glamour all I cared for;
I never bothered,' she said,
'With jars of powder or bottles of scent.
Now, when an unattractive
Elderly woman looks back at me from the mirror,
I splash this new perfume all over myself
And, if I close my eyes, I get the scent of love…
In the dark, the scent of love,' she said,
'And the smell of death.'

(LP)

Sunt lacrimae rerum

i gcuimhne Shéamuis Ennis

Sianaíl ag síofraí, geimhreata an gheoin,
Caoighol ag síomhná i bhfogus is fós
Siar go rinn duimhche, a Dhoinn, scaoil an sceol.

Súiste í uaill an druma mhóir, tarraing go tréan,
Dlúigh le gach buille ina chóir, tuargan an léin,
Taoiseach, iar n-ídeach don cheol, gabhann chun an chré.

Fásach gan cláirseach fadtharla an Teamhair 'na féar,
Go hanois, áfach, téarnamh ón éag
Níor chuaigh dár ndóchas; feasta tám tréith.

Ruaig ar lucht leasa agus bhró, mathshlua an aeir,
Gruagaigh na scairte i luísheol, chuchu an chíréip,
Grianáras Aonghusa ar Bhóinn spéirling do réab...

Tocht broinne an aithrígh bheir bláth ar bhachall droighin,
De shians chroit Oirféis an gallan cloiche rinc,
Ach, a ríphíobaire Éireann, clos duit ní dán arís
Choíche!

Sunt lacrimae rerum

In memory of Séamus Ennis

The fairy folk have raised a bitter cry, plangently they wail,
The banshees keen all through the night, and their anguished
    ululations
Disturb the western dunes where Donn, the death-god, rules in state.

Joyless the beat of the great bass drum, firmly struck with a flail,
The taut membrane vibrates and becomes a battery of pain;
The chief — now the music has ended — proceeds to his grave.

Tara has been long under grass, no harp is heard in the waste,
Up till now, however, we never lost hope that you'd escape
The menace of Death, but wiser and sadder we stand in dismay.

The hidden dwellers in rath and in fort have fled, they no longer
    feel safe;
Fled too are the hosts of the air, and the giants that used to sleep
    soundly in caves,
Aengus' sunlit palace by the Boyne has been ruined by the gale…

The exaltation of the penitent can make the old crozier blossom
    like a hedgerow in May;
The standing-stone danced to the tunes that Orpheus played:
But you, Prince of the Pipers of Ireland, are silenced for ever
    and always under the weight of clay.

(DS)

Paidir do Phádraig

A mhaicín na n-árann,
Atá eascartha in airde
Os chionn airde do mháthar,
Leanaim do rian chun na ráilleach:

Céim i gcoiscéim ar nós na lachan,
Ar nós mhuintir an Oileáin,
Ag iompar dom áireamh do bhcatha
Idir mo dhá láimh:

Mar bheadh uisce ó thobar an tslánaithe,
Gan ligint d'aon bhraon dul i bhásta…

Ar uair na hachaine
Agus an abhlann á hardach
Ardaím an tiomargain
Agus deinim m'ofráil uaim

Don gCoimirceoir síoraí:
D'fhonn glacadh leat faoina dhíon:
Éan coiligh ar bhíogadh don lá,
Fireanneach inchiolaraithe an áil…

Dod sheachaint ar stangadh roimh fhás,
Agus ar theip na ngrást,
Agus ar ghéaráin sa tslí,
Agus ar bheara faobhair,
Agus ar an uile dhrochní —

Nár lige Sé sinn i gcathaíbh!
    Amen.

Prayer for Patrick

Little son of my heart
Tall enough now
To tower over your mother,
I follow your path to the altar:

Step after awkward step,
Like the people of the Blasket,
Carrying the reckoning of your life
Between my hands:

Like water from the well of salvation,
And no drop wasted…

At the hour of entreaty
As the host is raised
I raise what I have gathered
And make my offering

To the eternal Protector:
That He accept you under His roof,
A cock at daybreak
The vulnerable male of the brood…

That He protect you from growth impaired
Or the failure of grace,
From rough stones along the way
From sharp edges
And from every evil —

May He not lead us into temptation.
      Amen.

(PS)

Cluichí páiste

Uamhan roimh phúcaí choinníodh sinn ag baile;
Is maith í mar ancaire an tine cois teallaigh:
'*Seo mo bhirín duit, birín beo, birín marbh!*' —
Ghlac uaithi an birín ach an deis níor thapaigh;
Idir mo dhá láimh an birín do cailleadh —
'*Beidh an trom, trom ort!*'

An trom, trom anois orm, is ní mar mhagadh!
Eagla púcaí is ea a ruaigeann amach mé,
Ar fán cois chladaigh nó le faobhar na haille —
Tine a chloíonn tine; don uaigneas ní taise.

Children's Games

We'd stay indoors for fear of the ghosts outside;
The fire on the hearthstone anchored us down fast:
'Here's a stick with a spark, let it live, let it die!' —
I took it in my turn but I'd missed my chance,
Before I could pass it on the spark had died —
'Load her with a heavy load!'

And now for sure my load is heavy!
Fear of the ghosts is what drives me abroad,
Astray on the shore or skirting the cliff:
Fire defeats fire, grief tempers grief.

(EC)

Pádraig roimh an mbál

I

Leithead na nguailne a bhain siar asam,
Mar níl sé fós i mbuaic a mhaitheasa:
Déanfaidh sé fás fós;
Ach na guailne sin,
Guailne fir iad
Roimh am.

Rós a thoibh sé an carabhat —
Féileacán ar ndóigh —
Agus seál póca den dath céanna,
Bróga nua agus gléas iontu,
An libhré eile haighreálta —
Casóg eireabaill a sheanathar,
A coinníodh dó,
Níor oir don bhfaisean.

Tráthnóna buí Bealtaine,
Taitneamh síoda ar an aer —
The mayfly is up!
Agus Pádraig ag dul ar rince.

II

Ar thalamh Nicaragua,
I scrogall an domhain tiar,
Tá comhaos Phádraig
Ag troid ar son an dúchais
Agus ar son na mbocht.
Óganach an tsoiscéíl
A dtug Críost grá dhó,
Rachmasach, álainn —

Patrick Getting Ready for the Ball

I

I was taken aback by the breadth of his shoulders,
Since he's not yet come into his prime:
He still has some growing to do;
But those shoulders,
They're the shoulders of a man
Before time.

A rose-coloured necktie he picked —
A butterfly of course —
And a handkerchief the same colour,
New shoes shining;
The rest of the gear is hired —
His grandfather's tail-coat,
Kept for him,
Doesn't go with the fashion.

A yellow May afternoon,
A silk shine on the air —
The mayfly is up!
And Patrick is off to the dance.

II

In Nicaragua,
In that distant neck of the world,
A boy of Patrick's age
Is fighting for his country
And its starving people.
Like the young man in the Gospel
That Christ declared his love for,
He was wealthy and good-looking —

Seinneann giotár —
Do chuala an forrán á chur air
Agus do ghluais —
Murab ionann is an fear samplach...
Do sheol 'uncail, an tAmbasadóir,
Buataisí nua saighdiúra
Chuige ó Washington.

A Íosa, níl iontu beirt ach garlaigh!
Cá n-iompód mo cheann
Go n-ćalód ón gcásamh?
Ón míréasún?
Conas is féidir liom mo thoil a chur
Le toil mo Dhé?

III

Gach lá dá maireann Pádraig
Is údar gairdeachais —
I Nicaragua,
Do ghléas an deartháir beag,
Iarmhar an áil,
Clown-suit air féin,
I leith is go ndíbreodh san
Buaireamh na muintire
Agus an sinsear as baile —
Níl ionam guíochtaint ar son mo bhuachalla,
Gan buachaill na máthar eile
A theacht im cheann.

He plays on the guitar —
When he heard the call
He enlisted at once —
Unlike his exemplar…
His Ambassador uncle
Sent him soldier's boots,
New from Washington.

Jesus, they're only children, the pair of them!
Where will I turn my head
To escape from lamentation,
From unreason?
How can I make my will
Conform to the will of my God?

III

Every day Pádraig lives
Is a cause of celebration —
In Nicaragua,
The little brother,
The last of the brood
Dressed up in a clown-suit
As if that would banish
The family's cares
While his older brother is away from home —
I cannot pray for my boy
Without recalling
That other mother's son.

(EC/DS)

Mutterrecht

Tá barraíocha mo mhéar
Lán de ghága, de ghearbacha;
Ní réitíonn an sobal leo.

Idir bhail agus bhinib
Cuimhním ar mo mháthair
Agus ar mo sheanamháthair;
Shaothraíodar araon lena ré…

D'fhonn ná teanntófaí
Sa chistin mise
Os chionn an dabhaigh ag níochán.

Mutterrecht

The tips of my fingers
All chapped and itchy,
Allergic to wash-up liquid.

Half-blessed, half-cursed,
I think how my mother
And grandmother,
Spent life in hard labour…

So that I'd not be a prisoner
In this kitchen
Washing dishes in the sink.

(LP)

Do Nuala Ní Dhomhnaill

Is í an mháthair áil í,
An craos.

Ní shásódh aon mholadh í
Dá mbeinn ag gabháil dó go lá dheireadh an tsaoil.

Is í an t-éamh í a chloiseann an leanbh istoíche
Laistíos dá chuimhne —
Riamh aniar ón dtráth san
'Nar baineadh é den gcín.

D'aithin sé é féin mar dhuine
Neamhspleách ar choimpléasc na máthar…

Ach leanann sise sa tóir air
Agus leanfaidh choíche:
Eagal leis í;
Eagal dó.

For Nuala Ní Dhomhnaill

She is the mother of them all,
She is appetite.

No praise is sufficient,
If I never stopped until kingdom come.

She is the scream the child hears at night
Underneath his memory —
Ever since he was weaned
From the breast.

He recognised himself as an individual
Separate from his mother's body...

But she keeps following him
And will never stop her pursuit;
He fears her;
So he should.

(LP)

Do mo bheirt leasiníon

Mar a bheadh dhá dhuilliúr ag rince ar an ngaoith,
Facathas dom mo leasiníonacha tamall sarar phósas a n-athair.

Le mac a bhí mo thnúth —
Má sea, d'aithníos 'na láthairsiúd
'Aeraí 's a leochailí de neacha iad cailíní beaga.

Bean acu cúldubh smaointeach, an bhean eile fionnagheal
    taodaoch:
Ar nós na bhfigiúr mbeag a chomharthaíonn an aimsear
    ar thigíní cipín ón Eilbhéis,
Theith siúr acu an doras isteach ach ar chorraigh siúr eile amach.

Chonac iad le súile a n-athar,
Níor ghleoite liom aon bheirt leanbh riamh ná iad:
Beirt ghearraphearsa, muirneach, muiníneach, muinteartha,
Lán d'éirim an ghrá…

Im shaol mar tá anois ann bíonn phéire dhe mhná óga:
Máithreacha clainne iad ag druidim i leith mheánaosta.
Is staidéartha go mór iad ná mise.
Orthu mo bhraith go léir ó cheann ceann na seachtaine,
Agus ó am go céile, de ruball fiarshúile, airím is mé ina n-aice
Mar a bheadh dhá dhuilliúr ag rince ar an ngaoith.

For My Two Stepdaughters

Like two leaves dancing in the wind,
I saw my stepdaughters shortly before I married their father.

I had longed for a son —
Even so, in their presence, I learned
Something of the giddiness and fragility of young girls:

One black-haired, thoughtful,
The other light blonde, impetuous:
Like little figurines that tell the weather
On the roofs of matchstick houses from Switzerland,
As soon as one sister stepped out the door, the other ran in.

I saw them through their father's eyes.
No two children were ever more beautiful to me:
Two miniature people, loving, confident, friendly,
Able for love...

In my life now there are two young women:
Mothers on the verge of middle age,
And much more sensible than I am.
I rely on them utterly from one end of the week to the next,
And, from time to time, from the corner of a squinting eye,
It seems, when I'm in their presence,
As if two leaves danced in the wind.

(LP)

Pianta cnámh

An stráice seo tinnis ó ghualainn go caol na láimhe
Ní mhaithfidh dom mo bheo.
Sloigim siogairlíní geala á dhíbirt;
Sean a chothaíonn siad é.

Ar nós an ainniseora sna meánaoiseanna
Agus na hailt á scaradh air,
Dá mb'eol dom cad ab áil leo,
Bhí sé ráite agam!

Ní chreidim sa leorghníomh,
Ní huasal liom an íobairt,
Is táim chomh traochta san
Ná haithneoinn an sceimhle —

Ach ródaíonn siad sa doircheacht,
Agus an fuadar san fúthu,
Lucht céasta mo sciatháinín mhartraithe
D'aon ghnó orm.

Aches

This pain that stretches from shoulder to wrist
Begrudges me my life.
I swallow bright jewels to banish it;
But they only make it worse.

Like the wretch in medieval times
Stretched on a rack,
If I knew what they wanted
I'd tell them!

I don't believe in reparation,
Or think suffering noble,
I'm so worn down
I'd not recognise terror —

But they take to the road in darkness,
Diligent about their business,
Twisting my crippled arm
Intent on inflicting pain.

(LP)

Maireann an tseanamhuintir

Thaithin leo an t-éadan ard ar mhnaoi —
Faisean an ghlibe ar bhaineannach ní bhfuair cion —
Agus scaradh leathan na súl
Agus an séanas mealltach chun tosaigh sa chár gléigeal:
Canóin na háilleachta ceapadh roimh theacht do Chríost…
Agus shamhlaíos dom féin go mbreacfainn a dtuairisc,
Mar, nuair nach ann dár nglúin-ne
Cé bhlaisfidh a séimhe siúd 'bhéascna?

Tharla mé ag múineadh scoile thiar ag an am san,
Agus ansan ar an mbinse leanbh mar lile:
Coimheascar na rós ar a leacain
Is a cúl dob órbhuí,
Gorm a rosca agus mall,
Caoincheart a braoithe,
Agus a béilín úr mar shú na gcraobh insa Mheitheamh.
Aon bhliain déag do chláraigh
Is splanc ní raibh ina cloigeann,
Ná í in aon chor 'na thinneas,
Ba leor bheith ann is bheith amhlaidh.

Tháinig an focal 'bé' i dtreis le linn teagaisc;
'Sin focal ná beidh agaibh,' do ráidh an mháistreás leo.
Phreab an lámh bheag in airde:
'Thá se agamsa'…
Íoróin throm an mhúinteora scaoileas den éill léi:
'Inis má sea don rang é, a Treas, a' stór do chuid eolais.'
Dána is teann as a gleoiteacht do raid sí an freagra:
'Bean gan aon éadach uirthi!'…
Do gháir Eoghan Rua.

A Survival

They liked a high forehead on a woman —
Never fond of a long fringe on a female face —
And the eyes set wide apart
And that enticing gap in the bright front teeth:
A canon of beauty going back beyond Christ...
And I imagined I would write their account,
For when our generation has passed
Who will value that subtle standard?

I happened to be teaching in Dunquin School at the time
And there on the bench a child like a lily:
The struggling rose on her cheek
And her head yellow as gold,
Blue her eyes and slow,
Slim and exact her eyebrows,
And her fresh mouth like raspberries in June.
Eleven years old in the register
And not a spark in her head,
It didn't distress her in the least;
Enough for her to be there and as she was.

The word 'muse' came up in the lesson;
'That's a word you won't know,' said the teacher.
The little hand flew up:
'I know it'...
I let slip a teacher's heavy irony:
'So tell the class, Therese dear, from your store of knowledge.'
Bold and firm in her beauty she shot back her answer:
'A woman with no clothes on!'
Eoghan Rua laughed.

(EC)

Briocht: Cathal Ó Searcaigh i gCorcaigh

Fáilte romhat aduaidh, a cheolghob,
Bláthaíonn an binse féd láimh,
Is anuas den bhfalla cromann mileanna dearga;
Deineann den halla an choill
Ina músclaíonn an maoilín,
An eilit ghlégheal —
Criostal iad mogaill na súl
Is a crúba den airgead —
Airíonn sí adharca na bhFiann,
Is de léim, í 'nár measc,
Eilit gheal na filíochta
Ar tinneall le beatha,
Is gur tuigeadh a *breed* bheith i ndísc —
Mo sheod thú! a Chathail,
Téagar na bhfann agus sult na ndearól,
I do dheasláimh beangán den gcaorthainn,
Ar sileadh le cloigíní óir!

Enchantment: Cathal Ó Searcaigh in Cork

Welcome from the North, then, song-bird,
The bench flowers under your hand,
And down from the walls cascade red blossoms;
The hall becomes a forest
Where wakes the little hornless doe,
The milk-white female deer —
Her eye-balls crystal
And her hooves silver —
She hears the horns of the Fianna,
And at one bound she is among us,
The white hind of poetry,
Pulsing with life,
And we thought that her breed was extinct —
My jewel you are, Cathal,
Strength of the weak and mirth of the destitute,
In your right hand a branch of rowan,
Hung with small golden bells!

(MM)

Miotas

Fé dhíon an tí seo
Ta cónaí ar na déithe:
Kore agus Dionysos:
Fíniúin sna locaí ag eisean,
Ise is a haprún lán 'bhláthanna.
Sna seanascéalta
A leithéid seo de theaghlach
Ba rogha leo:
Seanalánúin,
Two grey and aged snakes
That once were Cadmus and Harmonia…
Tógfaidh sé tamall uaim
Dul i gcraiceann na mionphearsan,
Mise, a shantaigh riamh lár stáitse…
Sna seanascéalta
Chuaigh an seantán tré thine;
Fuairthears ann
Luaithreach na gcnámh.

Myth

Under the roof of this house
The gods live:
Kore and Dionysos:
He with vines in his locks,
She with her apron of flowers.
According to legend
This is the kind of household
They liked:
An old couple,
Two grey and aged snakes
That once were Cadmus and Harmonia...
It'll take me some time
To get into the skin of the minor character —
I, who always craved centre-stage...
According to legend
The shack caught fire;
The ashes of their bones
Were found inside.

(CF)

Cearca

I

Is cuimhin liom binn dá gúna
    Idir mé agus na cearca:
Triantán dorcha éadaigh
    Mar a bheadh seol naomhóige,
Agus an pointe socair sa chosmas
    Gur mise é
Ag gliúcaíl dá dhroim
    Im portán sceimhlithe.

Ní bhíonn an *breed* sin de chearca ruadhearga
    Acu a thuilleadh:
Cearca chomh mór le muca,
    Caora tine acu in áit na súl,
Goib chorránacha, neamhthruamhéileacha orthu
    Agus camachrúba fúthu,
Innealta chun mé 'stolladh —
    Ní fheicim timpeall iad níos mó.

Bhí buataisí, leis, sa phictiúir
    Agus aprún garbh,
Ach caithim ailtireacht a dh'imirt orthusan
    Ar bhonn prionsabail,
Ní ritheann siad chugham
    Dá ndeoin —
'Ní cuimhin leat,' deir daoine, 'do sheanamháthair.'
    Is cuimhin, ón gcromán anuas.

II

I Saloinice, ina dhíbeartach,
    Saolaíodh an garsúinín;

Hens

I remember a fold of her dress
  Between me and the hens:
A triangle of dark cloth
  Like a sail on a currach
And the fixed point in the cosmos
  That I was
Peeping from behind it,
  A terrified crab.

That breed of reddish hens
  Has disappeared:
Hens as big as pigs,
  Balls of fire instead of eyes,
Hooked unmerciful beaks
  And twisted claws
Just right for tearing me —
  I don't see them around any more.

In the picture there were boots
  And a rough apron
But I have to build those in
  On the basis of principle,
They don't run towards me
  Of their own free will —
'You don't remember,' people say, 'your grandmother.'
  I do, from the hips down.

II

A refugee in Salonika
  The little boy was born

Banfhlaith de phór *Tatarin*
  Ba mháthair dó:
Bean choinleachta 'b ea í tráth
  I gcomplacht an *Tsarina*,
I gcúirt na m*buibhsíe liúidí*,
  I gcúirt na réamhdhaoine.

Throid 'athair le Deniken san Úcráin,
  Lean teideal captaein dó;
Críocha Gréag níor oir dó
  Mar altram don aoinghin:
Lofacht is stair na Meánmhara bréine
  Mhúch air an t-aer ann;
Tháinig 'na 'reachtaire cearc' go Cuileann,
  Cuileann an fhuachta, *Cold Collon*, in Éirinn.

'Does nobody here speak Greek?'
  Ars' an leanbh,
I mBéarla crochta na n-uasal
  Dar díobh é,
Ach lonnaigh 'na dhiaidh sin go sásta ar an bhfód
  Is, nuair a théadh dian air
Searmanas nósmhar an teaghlaigh,
  Dhein sé a ghearán leis na cearca!

Fiabhras a d'ídigh é,
  Fiabhras dóibh siúd
Ba bhreith báis ar óige
  Roimh *phenicillin*;
Oidhre na machairí résteipe anoir
  Síneadh i reilig os Bóinn;
Eaglais na hÉireann níor cheadaigh
  Cros an phápaire ar an uaigh.

To a princess of the race
        Of Tatarin:
She had been a lady in waiting
        In the company of the Tsarina
In the court of the *Buivshe Lyudy*
        The former people.

His father fought with Deniken in the Ukraine,
        Kept the title of Captain:
The land of Greece he found unfit
        For a nursery for his offspring;
The rotten age of the foul Mediterranean
        Smothered the air;
He came to Collon as a 'poultry steward'
        Cuileann an fhuachta, Cold Collon, in Ireland.

'Does nobody here speak Greek?'
        Said the child,
In the stiff upper-class English
        They all spoke
But later he settled happily on that ground
        And when he was oppressed
By the ceremonious rituals of the family
        He would complain to the hens!

Fever laid him low,
        One of those fevers that was
A death-sentence to the young
        Before penicillin;
The heir of the flat eastern steppes
        Lies in the graveyard by the Boyne.
The Church of Ireland would not permit
        A Papist cross on the grave.

III

Ní maith liom cearca —
      Bíonn boladh agus bús uathu —
Ach is maith liom an dá scéilín sin,
      Agus is ar chearca a bhraitheann siad.

III

I do not like hens—
        They are smelly and noisy—
But I like these two small stories,
        And they're both about hens.

(EC)

I leith na ruaidhe

Rabharta rua na hInide,
      Ruide i mbéal na trá,
Is an buinne fola fém easna
      Nach móide dhó aon lán...

Rua fós an luifearnach
      I mboireann an gharraí,
Rua liom teacht an Earraigh,
      Rua níochán do-ním...

Rua ceannacha an Mhárta,
      Rua Carghas im dháil,
Aiséirí rua is Aifreann
      Is éadach rua um Cháisc...

Rua barr críon an gheitire
      An uile thráth den mbliain
Is déanfaidh caipín cogaidh
      Don Dall a sháigh taobh Chríost.

Reddish

The russet springs of Shrove,
        Red mud at the mouth of the bay,
And the haemorrhage under my rib
        A long way from full-tide...

Russet the growth of weed
        In the burren of the yard,
Russet the Springtime's coming,
        Russet the wash I launder...

Russet the face of March,
        Russet is Lent upon us,
Red mass and resurrection,
        For Easter, russet raiment.

The rush's tip is russet
        Whatever be the season:
A war-cap for the Blind Roman
        Who pierced Christ's side.

(MM)

Shoa

ar fheiscint dhealbh chuimhneacháin íobairt na tine i Vienna dhom
— SAMHAIN 1988

An seanóir Giúdach ar a cheithre cnámha,
Ualach sneachta ar a ghuailne,
Cianta an rogha ina ghnúis —
'Mar seo,' adeir an t-íomhá miotail,
'Do sciúr mo chine "leacacha na sráide"
I Wien na hOstaire, leathchéad bliain ó shoin —
É sin agus ar lean é —
Ní náire feacadh i láthair Dé...

'Ach sibhse, na meacain scoiltithe,
'Bhur gcoilgsheasamh ar bhur "gcuaillí arda",
Níl agaibh teitheadh ón aithis:
Ársa na mBeann crapadh go hísle glún,
An Bheatha Ché insa láib,
Ar a chosa deiridh don mBrútach.'

Shoa

On seeing the memorial to the Holocaust in Vienna
— NOVEMBER 1988

The old Jew on his hands and knees,
A weight of snow on his shoulders,
Ages of election in his face —
'Thus,' says the graven image,
'My people scoured "the flagstones of the street"
In Vienna of Austria, fifty years ago —
That and what followed —
It is no shame to crouch in the face of God...

'But you, the forked root-vegetables,
Bolt upright on your "high stilts",
You shall not escape defilement:
The Ancient of the High Places stunted as low as the knee,
Eternal life in the mud,
The Brute on his hind legs.'

(MM)

'Fuair sí cuireadh na Nollag...'

do Nóra, d'éag 18 Nollaig 1989

Connlaigh fé iamh an teampaill ó ghoimh na haimsire
Agus ón éagumas cosanta —
Bás mná óige is taoscadh ar chuisle treibhe —
Cúb chughat féin le náire go bhfuil ag baile romhat
Do rós na ngarraithe, t'iníon, an cailín álainn,
Agus an lánú chomharsanta, ar sheomra folamh
Fillfidh, is ar aithleabaidh —
A n-eilit léimte!

'She was invited for Christmas...'

for Nóra, who died 18 December 1989

Huddle in the shelter of the church from the weather's
Depredations and your own impotence —
A young woman's death empties the blood of her people —
Cower in shame because your garden rose,
Your daughter, young and beautiful, is waiting for you at home,
While the other couple, your neighbours, will go back
To an empty room, and another bed —
Their young deer fled!

(LP)

Adhlacadh iníon an fhile

do Susie Iremonger

Comhthalán daoine críonna!
Léithe in aimhréití ar bhaitheas!
Droinn agus dathacha! Maoile!
Roic agus múchadh súl!
Scáil a n-óige ó aithne —
Foghlaim na dáimhe seo an bás.

Ach age bun altórach
San áit ar leagadh an chomhra
Tithe gloine an bhróin!
Raidhse dhathanna an Earraigh!
Gorm, buí agus rós!

Tá na driféaracha ag gol —
Éamh mar mheanaithe i gcroí —
Ach ins na fraitheacha in airde
Cloisim cloigín a gáire
Airgeadtha agus álainn.

Baineann seanaois le coiteann;
Roghnaigh sise a mhalairt.

The Burial of the Poet's Daughter

for Susie Iremonger

What an assembly of the old!
Of tangled grey hair!
Of stooped backs and rheumatism!
Of baldness, wrinkles and weak eyes!
Their youth unrecognisable now —
Experts at death this poetic band.

But at the base of the altar
Where the coffin was laid
The glass houses of sorrow!
The teeming colours of Spring!
Blue, yellow and rose!

The sisters are weeping —
Cries like an awl piercing the heart —
But high in the rafters
I hear the bell of her laughter
Silvered and beautiful.

Old age is the common fate;
She chose the opposite.

(PS)

Moment of truth

'Bhfuil ciall in aon chor le bheith beo, a Mháire?'
         Ceist orm 'gem dheirfiúirín…
Ní deirfiúirín a thuilleadh anois í
Ach bean bhreá, bhláfar —
              Baintreach í agus máthair,
              Thar líne na gréine gafa —
              Ach domhsa fós an deirfiúirín…
Bhíodh an cheist chéanna ag ár máthair,
Bean ba gheanúla is ba thréithí
          Dá dtáinig —
          Is ar a shon san…
Agus an bhean úd Gaeltachta,
A mhúin dom bean seach bainirseach —
            'An ann do Dhia, a Mháire?'
            A deireadh…
Am briathar féin ná feadar
Ach nach mór dom creideamh na gcomharsan
Mar mhapa chun go mbreacfainn marc air
            Agus an marc a bheith 'na chloch thagartha…
'Bhfuil mo mheabhair ag teip, a Mháire?'
Má tá, ní galar aoinne amháin é.

Moment of truth

'Is there any sense in being alive, Máire?'
        My little sister asked me...
No longer a little sister
But a fine woman in her prime —
        Widow, and mother,
        Past the flush of youth —
        But still my little sister...
Our mother, the most loving and accomplished woman
Who ever lived
        Had the same question —
        And still...
And that Gaeltacht woman
Who taught me 'a woman is not a seal' —
        'Is there a God, Máire?'
        She'd say...
Upon my oath I don't know
But I need the neighbours' faith
As a map to leave a mark on
        And that mark a boundary stone.
'Am I losing my mind, Máire?'
If she is, she's not the only one.

(CF)

Leagan ar sheanará

fuair Bríde Ní Chíobháin, ná maireann, an rá atá i gceist
óna huncail Séan Ó Cíobháin, saoi

'Sagairt is bráithre! Is d'imigh an bhairdne eatarthu!'
'Bairnigh' a bhíodh á rá coitianta agus scéalta ag tacú leis;
Ach bhí fios a mhalairt agatsa agus dúraís é;
D'éistíodar gan trasnaíl leat, ach níor athraigh a dtuairim,
Agus bhreac an scoláire síos uathusan é, agus ní uaitse...

Ambaic! Ba mhaith é t'eolas;
Cruinnchomhaireamh nath ár n-aithreacha
D'áirís ó ló go ló dúinn,
Gan dóchas puinn, á n-aithris duit,
Go dtuigfí tú ar fónamh
Ná go mbeadh an scéal 'na cheart againn;
Ní rabhais i dtaoibh le dóchas
I muilte brón na beatha crua,
    A Bhríde.

Monbhar solamanta sodair fút,
Ar fud a' tí,
Líon de phobalghuth an t-ionad san
Ba láthair suímh
Don aspalacht a chleachtais chughainn
Is dod bhainistí,
Agus diamhaireacht na salm san
Níor chuaigh i ndísc
Ó chaithis suas ar maidin ort
Gur shínis siar —
Níteá do chorp Dé Sathairn i gcomhair an Domhnaigh;
Bhí seál den *mohair* agat
Agus chaiteá stocaí...
    Gabhaimse orm!

A New Edge on an Old Saw

*The late Bríde Ní Chíobháin learned the saying that is
referred to from her uncle Seán Ó Cíobháin*

'Priests and friars between them caused the demise of the Muses.'
Mussels, not Muses, was their name in the corrupt local expression
And the wildest stories were improvised to make it seem credible:
'Priests and friars between them caused the demise of the Mussels!'

But you were the wisest, the only one to recite it correctly:
Priests and friars between them caused the demise of the Muses.
People listened politely but no one revised their opinion
And a man who could write neatly inscribed the corrupt version
       in permanent ink.

God help us! You had the learning:
All the ancestral lore
You related to us day by day
Without any hope your narration
Would be rightly understood
Or saved by us for posterity;
It was not hope you relied on
In the dark mills of this harsh world,
       Dear Bríde!

Your solemn murmuring as you bustled
Through the house,
Filled it with a congregation of voices,
Made it holy ground
For the ministry you practised in our midst.
Your gospel of thrift
And the mysteriousness of those psalms
Never abated
From the time you threw on your clothes in the morning

'Mo ghraidhn é an té 'tá ag titim libh,
A chipe amhas!
Ceaintíní agus crosa, mhuis,
Do bhuair mo mheabhair!
Fasan amach fém chosa uaim,
'S ná liathaigh mo cheann,
   A Diúile!'

Fada do dhuanaireacht 'na tost,
Aidhe mo léir!
An spadhar 'na shuan, is do cholainn bhocht
Ag tabhairt an fhéir;
Ach déanfair c'leachta dhomsa anocht
Is le fad mo ré:
Beirt bhaineannach go fileata
Ag dul 'on chré,
A n-allagar gan ainbhfios,
Is gan uamhan roimh chléir —
   Dar mo leabhar breac!

Till you lay down at night —
On Saturday you washed all over to be ready for Sunday;
You had a shawl of mohair
And you used to wear stockings…
     I declare!

God help whoever has to look after you,
You pack of hooligans!
With your pranks and escapades
You have me driven demented!
Get out from under my feet,
Or you'll turn my hair grey,
     Yeh! Julia! You…!

Your lilting and crooning have long been silenced,
My heart still aches!
Your angers are at rest, and your pitiful body
Rots in the grave;
But you'll be my companion tonight
And all the rest of my days:
Two females alive in their imagination,
Turning into grass,
No limits to their eloquence
And no fear of the clergy —
     I swear to God!

(DS)

I leaba an dearúid, an tarcaisne

'Ní mhaireann cuimhne air anso,' arsa fear na féasóige,
'Ach mar dhuine des na boic mhóra,
Mar dhuine den lucht rachmais' —

Thusa nár fhan riamh agat
Dhá phingin rua ded thuarastal
A chuimileofá dá chéile!

Is dócha go mbíonn *begrudgers*,
Clann an doichill, clann Lóbais,
Ins gach aon pharóiste;
Is minic duine acu ina chliamhain isteach.

Fé mar chlúdaigh
Ciúbanna gránna suimint'
Na seanaláithreacha,
Fé mar tháinig screamh an Bhéarla
Ar uaisleacht na canúna,
Chuaigh insint scéil ort i ndísc, a Bhrúnaigh,
Sa cheantar a roghnaís ód chroí —
Sin é an saol, a dhuine —
Níor bhásaís go dtí anocht.

Ach cuimhnímse ort i mbláth do mhaitheasa,
Nuair a thaibhsigh glóire na hintilíochta ót éadan
Agus muintearas agus greann ód chontanós,
Nuair gur rángaís ins an dúthaigh seo
Ar do chomh-mhaith de chomhleacaithe,
Sea, agus ar do chomh-mhaith de mháistrí —
Féach, gur 'thogair na Danair i mbrogaibh na dáimhe isteach',
A dhream gan iúl gan aithne,
Gur náir libh bhur muintir féinig!

Not Forgotten: Disparaged

'Nobody remembers him here,' said the bearded fellow,
'Except, maybe, as one of the big shots,
A prominent member of the propertied classes' —

You who never had enough
Of your salary left to rub
Two brown pennies together!

Probably there are begrudgers,
Curmudgeons and churls galore
To be found in every parish;
Often they've married into a farm.

Just as old homesteads
Have been replaced
By ugly cubes of cement,
And a scum of broken English
Has coated our noble tongue,
Your story, Father Browne, is being obliterated
In the district closest to your heart —
That's how it goes, I tell you —
You didn't die till tonight!

But I remember you in your prime,
When the power of the intellect shone from your face
And the play of your features promised friendly diversion
When you met in this countryside
People who were your compeers —
Yes, and people that could match you as mentors —
But now, *'boors have usurped the thrones of the poets'* —
You stupid unschooled rabble,
Ashamed of your own ancestors!

Tá siadsan san úir anois
A dtiocfadh uathu focal do chosanta:
An cailín daortha san éagóir,
Cléireach an Teampaill seo,
An slua 'bhailíodh gach oíche chughat ar an gCill:
Comharsana meabhracha ba mhaith i mbád is ar ghort,
Nár dheoranta iad do shaíocht na cruinne,
Ach a mhúin duit conas
An tsaíocht sin a ghléasadh i gculaithirt na Gaelainne:
Fathaigh a dtáinig abhaigh orthu mar shíolbhach!

Thána anso
Le cloch a chur id leacht,
A shagairt uasail:
Bead ag imeacht anois,
Is ní móide go deo
Go bhfillfead.
Is fearr a mhaireann tú im chroí is im intinn
Ná in aon leac greanta ar fhalla.
Rud gan anam an leac,
Ach is lasair bheo é an Spiorad Naomh —
Lonraíonn mar a bhfuil 'éirim.
Má b'é seo tráth mo bhaile,
Táim gan baile feasta.

They are all dead now
Those who'd have spoken up in your defence:
That girl who had been wrongly slandered,
The man who had been the Clerk of this Chapel,
The crowd that gathered each night in your house at the Cill:
Discerning neighbours, adept with oar and spade,
And in no way at a loss on the paths of learning —
Did they not teach you how
To transform that learning into the beauty of their native Irish? —
They were giants whose descendants turned out to be dwarfs!

I came here
To lay a stone on your cairn,
Distinguished priest —

I will be going now
And it's unlikely
That I'll ever return.

You are more alive in my heart and mind
Than in any plaque fixed to a wall;
There is no soul in a stone —

But the Holy Spirit is a living flame
That will shine wherever it chooses —

If this was once my home,
From this out I am homeless.

(DS)

Tigh Mhóire ag caoineadh Shéamuis

Do thugadar Séamus na Cille abhaile
I mboiscín luaithrigh go scéitheadh na haille,
Fé bhun na Cille, mar 'deineadh é 'leathadh,
D'fhógraíodar séala ar scéala a bheatha.

Ar chuimhnigh éinne ar an leanbh mánla,
Buachaillín álainn, oscailte, grámhar,
A thaithigh an ceantar riamh fé áthas
Ó d'iompar 'na bhunóc ann ar dtúis é a mháthair?

Áilteoir ainglí, rógaire saonta,
Do chuir sé scoil agus rang trí chéile,
Níor chaill sé riamh é, go deireadh a laethanta,
Ní raibh aon pheaca riamh ar Shéamus.

Is d'fhás sé suas in' óigfhear déanta,
Do rincfeadh seit is do dhein cúirtéireacht,
Ba mhaith i mbád é, ar chnoc is ar aonach,
Ba mhaith ag caint é is b'fhearr ag éisteacht.

Do fuair sé a chantam de bhráca an tsaoil seo
Is a chantam ratha, mar 'bhí: dea-chéile,
Thóg beirt iníon ba ghleoite i bhféachaint,
Sin triúr ag gol go fuíoch á éamais.

Dochtúir fónta, comrádaí tréitheach,
Níor cheil sé cabhair ná leigheas ar aon neach,
Is mó san oíche a chiorraigh 'ár n-éineacht,
I dtábhairne an ghrinn 's ar thinteán na féile.

Níorbh é a dhearmad riamh an taobh so
Dá fhaid ó bhaile a lean sé 'éirim,

Tigh Mhóire Grieving for Séamus

It was the last homecoming of Séamus na Cille:
They carried his urn from the church to the cliff-top
And scattered his ashes in sad valediction —
His life now over and his sins forgiven.

Did anyone think of the boy in his cradle,
That gentle child, so frank and engaging,
Who was charmed by this place from the very first day
His mother brought him here in her arms as a baby?

Half-angel, half-prankster, now simple, now cute,
He threw teachers and pupils into utter confusion —
He never lost it, even after his schooling;
But you couldn't blame Séamus, half-innocent, half-fool!

A captivating fellow when he came of age;
He'd dance a set, be friendly or flirtatious —
Completely at ease in boat, field or fair —
He talked persuasively and listened gravely.

The harrows of living did not leave him unscathed
But a kind, loving wife was rich compensation;
Two beautiful eye-catching daughters they raised —
Three women left desolate to weep and to pray.

A capable doctor and friendly host,
His services and skills impartially bestowed;
Many a night he made the darkness sparkle
In the inviting pub and by the lively hearthstone.

He never forgot this corner of Eden
Although in exile he'd to pursue his career:

Dob iad a mhuintir ár muintir féinig,
Na seanfhondúirí a mhúin dó an Ghaelainn.

A Dhia 'tá thuas, mar seo ár n-éileamh,
Glac chughat Séamus i measc na naomh geal,
Réitíodh Gobnait an párlús féin dó
I dteannta an tslua bheannaithe as Éirinn…

Suaimhneas síoraí go raibh ar 'anam!
Is cuimhne ar Dhún Chuinn leis fós sna Flaithis!
Ó éirí gréine os chionn an Chlasaigh
Go dul 'na luí dhi fé iarthar mara.

Scaiptear an t-iarsma ar mhuir 's ar thalamh,
Sin sínte ar an ngaoith dá thaisí feasta.
B'shin mar ba mhian leis is é 'na bheathaidh
An turas deireanach a thabhairt abhaile.

Its people were our people,
Those elders who taught him true Munster speech.

O God above, we beg Thy benison,
Let Séamus na Cille be sainted in heaven;
May St Gobnait herself have his room made ready
In the mansion that is destined for Ireland's blessed.

May his soul be granted eternal peace
And the Heavens be bright with the light of Dún Chuinn —
From the time the sun shines on the Clasach's cheek
Till it sinks in the depth of the darkening sea.

Scatter the remains over ocean and isthmus,
His last traces will float on the wind.
That's what he'd wished for, all the years of his living —
This final journey to the fields of his infancy.

(DS)

Do Mhaoilre (dá ngoirtear Milo)

Balcaire beag stóinsithe,
    Meidhreach, mánla, gáireatach,
Diabhailín is aingilín
    I mburla amháin fáiscithe…
Éadromaíonn an croí ionam
    Ar theacht duit ar an láthair,
Is cuirim fad mo ghuí leat
    Trí phóirsí an lae amáirigh.

Mo ghraidhn go deo do mháthair dheas,
    Í gleoite, geanúil, álainn,
Mo ghraidhnse fós é t'athair dil
    A d'oileas féin 'na pháiste;
Fuil theasaí na hAfraice,
    Fionnuaire an iarthair ársa,
Do cumascadh id cholainnín
    Chun ratha is chun sláinte.

Fáilte fáidh is file romhat,
    A mhaoinín bhig na fáistine,
Buaic is coróin ár n-achaine,
    Mar 'léitear ins na trátha;
Uile chion ár mbaochais
    Go soirbhe it fhás tú!
Planda beag iolfhréamhach tú
    Thug toradh os chionn gach áirimh.

To Maoilre (Known as Milo)

Stocky little fellow, so
      Merry, gentle, jolly;
Little devil and angel
      Squeezed into one bundle,
My heart lightens
      When you come near,
And I send all my wishes with you
      Through the porches of tomorrow.

All praise to your sweet mother
      Delightful, loving, beautiful,
And your beloved father
      I taught myself when he was a boy;
The hot blood of Africa
      And the coolness of the ancient west
Come together in your little body
      For grace and health.

A prophet's welcome to you, and a poet's,
      Little gift foretold,
The climax and crown of our entreaty
      Recited in our daily prayers,
May every part of our gratitude
      Ease you as you grow!
You're a many rooted plant
      Flowering beyond all measure.

(PS)

Dán próis do Inigo

Beirt mhac atá agem' mhacsa:
Prionsa óg é an sinsearach,
Balcaire beag stóinsithe an driotháirín,
Ceithre bliain eatortha.

Níl an feairín beag cainteach,
Cé go bhfuil dhá bhliain scoite aige.
No! agus *Why?* iad an dá fhocal is mó a thaitníonn leis,
Agus an bhéic aige, scoiltfeadh sí do cheann
Nuair is míshásta dhó.

Níl sé i spleáchas éinne:
Bain do shúil de is ealóidh sé,
Amach thar geata le haer an tsaoil,
Taise ghiobalach de choinín cniotáilte fén' ascaill,
Gaiscíoch tiomanta é, ar eachtra theanntásach.

Leanaimse, an mháthair áil é, sa tóir go discréideach,
Idir gháire agus bhuaireamh im aigne,
Isteach fé scáth na gcrann.
Aithníonn sé ag teacht mé is cromann ar rith,
A dhá cholpa bheaga, bheathaithe, ag imeacht ar nós na loine.

I ndeireadh na feide tagaimse suas leis,
Caitheann é féin ar a chúl ar an bhfód
Agus gach scairteadh gáire as —
Tá an bua aige.

Stánann trí bhreacarsach na nduilliúr in airde,
Idir é féin agus léas, go sásta.
Léimeann an t-éan de chraobh os a chionn,

Prose Poem for Inigo

My son has two sons,
Four years between them.
The older one is a prince,
His brother a sturdy buck.

The little one is not given to talk
Even though he's two years old.
No! and *Why?* are his favourite words.
And when he's not happy
His roar would take the head off you.

He doesn't depend on anyone:
Take your eye off him and he's away
Out over the gate, free as a breeze,
A raggedy woollen rabbit under his oxter,
A dedicated hero venturing boldly.

I, the mother hen, follow at a discreet distance,
Torn between laughter and worry,
In under the shade of the trees.
He sees me coming and runs for it,
His chubby little legs churning like pistons.

And when I do catch up with him
He throws himself on the ground,
The laughter spilling from him
As he savours his victory.

He stares happily through the tangle of leaves
That shield him from the light.
The bird leaps from a branch above him,

Síneann an leanbh méar údarásach —
'Birr', adeir sé le fonn, 'Birr, Birr'.

The child stretches out an authoritative finger —
'Birr', he sings, 'Birr, Birr'.

(PS)

Nec patris linquens dexteram

Ar deire thiar dhein éan de —
Peata éin.
Chruinnigh éanlaith na coille ag an bhfuinneoig,
Ag faire air á bheathú —
Bhain grásta leis an uain sin,
Le radharc na spéire agus
Le humhlú na gcrann fén ngaoith —
Le mo sheanduine, le mo leanbh fir.

Not Letting Go the Father's Right Hand

At the end he became a bird,
A pet bird.
The wild birds gathered at the window,
To watch him fed —
That was a time of grace,
With the wide sky and
The trees bowing in the wind —
My old love, my man-child.

(MM)

Máiréad

Bhí sí i gcónaí tostach ar maidin,
Ar nós Mheiriceánaigh mhná ná fuair a cupán caifé.
Niombas mar luan láich uirthi an tost san,
An bhuaintseasamhacht, an ciúineas, go dtí go mbriseann
Uirthi a gean gáire; ritheann drithleoga solais
Ar fuaid na láithreach. Is í aeráid an teaghlaigh í,
Caoin, suáilceach, dea-oibreach, ár ndúnáras iontruist.

Margaret

She was always silent in the morning,
Like an American woman denied her cup of coffee.
Like a hero-light about her head, the nimbus of silence,
Of steadfast quietness, until she breaks
Into sweet laughter; light sparkles and runs
Through the room. She is the climate of this house,
Benevolent, gentle, obliging, our fortress sanctuary.

(LP)

Ceann bliana

Cóirím mo chuimhne chun dulta dhi 'on chré,
Fillim spíosraí san eisléine léi agus airgead cúrsach;
Tá sneachta fós ar ithir na cille,
Sínim le hais an choirp ar mo leabaidh.

One Year After

I arrange my memory in readiness for the grave,
Put spices in her shroud and silver coins;
The snow is still on the cemetery ridge;
I lie down beside the body on my bed.

(LP)

Mo chumha

Do scoith mo chumha mé ar an gconair —
Thóg sé tamall uaidh teacht suas liom,
Moillíonn sé anois —
Ciorraíonn sé an bóthar dom.

Regret

Regret passed me on the path —
It took him a while to catch up;
Now he slows down —
It takes two to shorten the road.

(LP)

'Táim cinnte, ó thaobh eolaíochta de, aon rud a bhí agamsa sa bh-
filíocht, bhí sé á rá in ait éigin. Ní ón mbroinn a fuaireas é; chuala é.'

— MÁIRE MHAC AN TSAOI (*INNTI* 8, 1984, 41)

Ón uair go mbraitheann go leor d'éifeacht a cuid filíochta ar chúrsaí
fuaime, is minic a chleachtann Máire Mhac an tSaoi litriú focal nach
bhfuil ag teacht ar fad leis an gCaighdeán Oifigiúil. Nuair a scarann
sí leis an gCaighdeán de ghnáth, is mar mhaithe le meadaracht é, nó
le go dtuigfidh an léitheoir conas a déarfaí focal áirithe i gcanúint
Chorca Dhuibhne. In áiteanna eile, leanann sí nósanna litrithe a bhí
i bhfeidhm nuair a scríobhadh na dánta. Mar áis don léitheoir, tugtar
anso thíos cuid de na leaganacha neamhchaighdeánacha a úsáidtear
sa leabhar seo agus an leagan caighdeánach taobh le gach ceann acu.

A fhir dar fhulaingeas	'duí'	duibhe
Ceathrúintí Mháire Ní Ógáin	'a phréa'cha'	a phréamhacha
An bhean mhídhílis	'díthi'	di
Cam Reilige	'ar chiosaíbh'	ar chiumhaiseanna
An fuath	'ar dhu'í gain'í'	ar dhuimhche gainmhe
Fód an imris:		
Ard-Oifig an Phoist 1986	'ruchar'	urchar
	'Olltaigh'	Ultaigh
	Kranz	geáitsí
	'do ráidhis é'	a dúirt tú é
Codladh an ghaiscígh	'fém' borlach'	faoi mo bhrollach
	'spíonóig'	spúnóg
	'luan láich'	luan laoich
Do phatalóigín gearrchaile	'chéil'	cheil
Ceangal do cheol pop	'it ampar'	dod iompar
Fómhar na farraige	'an mh'rúch'	an mhurúch

Amach san aois	'nódh'	nua
Paidir do Phádraig	'i gcathaíbh'	i gcathú
Pianta cnámh	'sean'	is ea
Maireann an tseanamhuintir	'do ráidh'	a dúirt
Miotas	'fuairthears'	fuarthas
Cearca	buibhsíe liúidí	na ndaoine a bhí (Rúisis)
	'bean choinleachta'	bean choimhdeachta
Adhlacadh iníon an fhile	'age'	ag
Moment of truth	'gem'	ag mo
Leagan ar sheanará	'fasan'	ſáᵹ (an áit) as san
	'Diúile'	Julia
	'c'leachta'	cuideachta

Where alternative versions of individual poems have been previously published, the version included in this collection is that preferred by the author.

Do Shíle

Valentine Iremonger's translation has been previously published under the title 'I remember a room on the seaward side'.

Ceathrúintí Mháire Ní Ógáin

The poem was originally composed as a series of freestanding shorter poems, modelled on early Irish sagas where the central characters engage in poetic conversation at heightened moments in the narrative.

An dá thráigh

This is the opening poem in the 1973 collection *Codladh an Ghaiscígh* but was conceived as an epilogue to 'Ceathrúintí Mháire Ní Ógáin'.

Cian á thógaint díom

Originally included in *Shoa agus Dánta Eile*, it has been relocated in the interest of thematic continuity.

An fuath (1967)

Written for a political cabaret in New York organised by John Arden as a protest against the Vietnam war.

Fód an imris: Ard-Oifig an Phoist, 1986

'A National Day of Commemoration was instituted in 1986 to occur on the anniversary of the date in 1921 that a truce was signed ending the Irish War of Independence. It commemorates all Irish men and women who died in past wars or on service with the United Nations.

The quotation from Máire's father, Seán MacEntee, is taken from a public letter he wrote to the *Irish Times* in 1970, following a gun-battle at St Michael's Church, West Belfast' (note provided by Douglas Sealy). This poem was originally published in *Shoa agus Dánta Eile* (1999) but has been included here after 'Cam reilige 1916–1966' in the interests of thematic continuity.

Iníon a' Lóndraigh

The epigraph is from the following quatrain by Piaras Feirtéar:

> Is deas an baile é Baile na Lóndrach,
> Is gurb os a chionn a shoilsíos an ghrian,
> Is go bhfuil comharartha cille ar Inín a' Lóndraigh
> Os cionn sál a bróige thiar!

Love has pitched his mansion

The title is from Yeats's 'Crazy Jane talks to the bishop':

> A woman can be proud and stiff
> When on love intent;
> But Love has pitched his mansion in
> The place of excrement;
> For nothing can be sole or whole
> That has not been rent.

The italicized lines in the original poem echo the words of Pontius Pilate as given in 'Caoineadh na maighdine'.

Sunt lacrimae rerum

The title is from line 462 of Book 1 of Virgil's *Aeneid*, 'sunt lacrimae rerum et mentem mortalia tangent', 'the world is a world of tears, and the burdens of mortality touch the heart'.

Cluichí páiste

The full verse from which the lines in italics are drawn is:

> Seo mo bhirín duit,
> Birín beo, birín marbh.
> Má fhaigheann mo bhirín bás
> Idir do dhá láimh,
> Beidh an trom, trom ort!

The verse was spoken as accompaniment to a children's game in which a lighted piece of kindling was passed from one child to the next until extinguished. The child holding the wood when the flame went out was deemed to have lost the game and was set upon by the others.

Miotas

The italicised lines are from Matthew Arnold's 'Cadmus and Harmonia':

> And there, they say, two bright and aged snakes,
> Who once were Cadmus and Harmonia,
> Bask in the glens or on the warm sea-shore,
> In breathless quiet, after all their ills;
> Nor do they see their country, nor the place
> Where the Sphinx lived among the frowning hills,
> Nor the unhappy palace of their race,
> Nor Thebes, nor the Ismenus, any more.

Cearca

During her time in the Department of External Affairs, Máire was sent by Minister Frank Aiken, along with Conor Cruise O'Brien and two other officials, to learn Russian from a family of Russian immigrants who had settled in Collon, County Meath. The story referred to in the second section of the poem concerns that family's experience in Russia and in Ireland.

Shoa

The phrases in italics are taken from 'Caoineadh na maighdine'.

Moment of truth

The line 'a mhúin dom bean seach bainirseach' means literally 'who taught me the difference between a woman and a female seal'. A corresponding phrase in English might be the expression 'she is the cat's mother' as an admonishment to a child for using the word 'she' inappropriately. For the sake of thematic coherence, the order in which 'Moment of truth' and 'I leaba an dearúid, an tarcaisne' appear in *Shoa agus Dánta Eile* has been reversed here.

I leaba an dearúid, an tarcaisne

The phrase 'Clann Lóbais' might be translated as 'Philistines', a generic term of abuse for the *nouveaux riches* whose recently acquired social status is undermined by cultural ignorance and intellectual inferiority. In the seventeenth-century prose satire *Pairlement Chloinne Tomáis*, Clann Thomáis, the low-born upstarts who have little regard for the bardic traditional of learning, are descended from Lobus. The line 'thogair na Danair i mbrogaibh na dáimhe isteach' is taken from poem No. 61 in *Burdúin Bheaga* (1925), a collection of epigrammatic short poems from early modern Irish edited by Tomás Ó Rathile.

Tigh Mhóire ag caoineadh Shéamuis

'Tigh Mhóire (the House of Mór) is a spot near Vicarstown in the parish of Dunquin in west Kerry. According to local tradition the goddess Mór of Munster is buried there. Cill Ghobnait (the Church of Gobnait) is the site of the old church near the cliff northwest of Dunquin. The late Mgr Pádraig de Brún had a small house built there that was known as Tigh na Cille because it was within the boundaries of the old site. His sister's three children who stayed there in holiday time were given the soubriquet of 'na Cille'. The Clasach is that part of Mount Eagle where the old road from Ventry to Dunquin crossed the ridge' (note provided by Douglas Sealy).

Nec linquens dexteram patris
The title is from a hymn entitled 'Verbum supernum prodiens', attributed to St Thomas Aquinas, and traditionally sung during the Feast of Corpus Christi.

Born in Dublin in 1922, Máire Mhac an tSaoi is the daughter of the politician and author Seán MacEntee (the anglicized form of her name) and niece of the scholar and translator Monsignor Pádraig de Brún (Patrick Browne). Her mother Margaret Browne MacEntee was a Lecturer in Irish at University College Dublin. Mhac an tSaoi spent long periods in the Kerry Gaeltacht around Dunquinn in County Kerry during her childhood, where her name is still on the local school roll. She was educated at Alexandra College and Loreto College, before going on to study Irish, French, and English at University College Dublin. Following her graduation, she spent two years at the School of Celtic Studies in the Dublin Institute of Advanced Studies. She studied law at King's Inns, and, in 1944, became the first Irish woman to be called to the bar. In 1945, she went to Paris on a travelling studentship from the National University of Ireland, and spent the following two years as a postgraduate student in the *Institute des Hautes Études* at the Sorbonne.

From 1947 to 1962, she served in the Irish diplomatic corps, in Dublin, Strasbourg, and Madrid, in Africa and America, and at the United Nations. She also spent a number of years working with lexicographer Tomás de Bhaldraithe on his English-Irish dictionary. In 1962 she married Conor Cruise O'Brien, and became step-mother to three children from his previous marriage, Kate, Fedelma, and Dónal. The couple adopted two children of their own, Pádraig and Máiréad (Patrick and Margaret).

Her debut volume, *Margadh na Saoire* (1956), was followed by *Codladh an Ghaiscígh agus Véarsaí Eile* (1973), *An Galar Dubhach* (1980), *An Cion go dtí Seo* (1987), and *Shoa agus Dánta Eile* (1999). She has also published two scholarly works, *Dhá Sgéal Artúraíochta* (1946) and *Cérbh í Meg Russell?* (2007), a novella, *A Bhean Óg Ón...* (2001), a collection of Irish translations from the English of Pádraig de Brún, *Miserere* (1971), *A Heart Full of Thought* (1959), which contains translations from Classical Irish, and *Trasládáil* (1997) a bilingual miscellany of poems in Irish with her own translations. Her autobiography, *The Same Age as the State*, appeared in 2003.

She was poet-in-residence at University College Dublin (1991–1992) and was Associate Fellow at the National Humanities Center in Durham, North Carolina in 1995. Her honours and awards include the O'Shaughnessy Poetry Award (1988) and an honorary doctorate in Celtic Studies from the National University of Ireland (1992). In 2004 she was appointed Honorary Professor of Irish Studies at NUI Galway.

She lived for many years on the summit of Howth Head outside Dublin, and now lives with her daughter in Co. Meath.